—EMAIL REPLIES FROM FRIENDS & FAMILY—

"You [Jarrett] continue to be such an inspiration. When I learned your trail-name, I said out loud how perfect that is for you. You are on such an amazing journey, the kind of journey that few of us have the courage to undertake, and even fewer know how to listen to. Your soul, I truly believe, is an old one. You are a man of peace, and I am, again, honored to be included in your circle." —*Margi Marsett (Thursday, May 16, 2002)*

"Jarrett, the stories you share with us are just incredible. So inspiring! Honestly, I can't stop raving about you. Can't even say enough about what a pot of gold you are. So rich in beauty, in generosity, always willing to share—you are out there somewhere, where people follow the map to search you out and yearn for your stories so we can indulge. You have been my anchor Jarrett. Helping to keep me grounded and learning how beautiful life is, even during those difficult times. I thank you for sharing and I thank you for believing in yourself to make this journey a life growth for you in your heart and soul. You are giving yourself the biggest gift a person can receive!" —*Kim Barone (Monday, June 10, 2002)*

"After looking down this email list [of friends and family] I see that I don't know many of you, so I guess it's fair to say that many of you don't know me. However we all have a common bond. Every few days, or sometimes weeks, we get updates on Jarrett's journey, and I (after a rough day), wanted to share some thoughts. I studied abroad with Jarrett in Spain about 5 years ago, and we've been good friends ever since. Like I mentioned before, I don't know many of you, so I don't know where you actually read Jackie's [Jarrett's sister] emails. What I do know is where I read them. I work for a hedge fund in midtown. I have no windows in my office, and because I have to track every move of the stock market, I can't leave my computer screen at all during the day (except to take a piss, maybe). So I can't tell if it's sunny, cloudy, raining or snowing outside until I leave at about 6pm. Most of my days are filled with lots of yelling, staring, and everything involved is usually pretty stressful and very intense. However, whenever I get a Jarrett report, and read about him trekking through the mountains, hanging by a river or camping under the stars, I take a second and I envision this longhaired, bearded, freak of a man, who must smell so bad by now, and I laugh. I nod my head to him, and I, even if it's for a brief moment, I am on the trail with him. And those few seconds out there with him, believe it or not, gets me through the rest of my day. So Jarrett my friend, you are a good man, keep pushin' and thanks."
—*Matthew Plotkin (Tuesday, June 25, 2002)*

"Although your [Jarrett's] physical journey is not over, I clearly see that you have reached enlightenment, and that is the ultimate goal! I told you awhile ago that I thought I could learn from you and then you decided to venture out on this amazing challenge…you are right, words cannot describe. When I did the AIDSRide, I had similar feelings. It took me months to write my sponsors the thank you letters, and it still wasn't all that great. I'm not the best at expressing myself with words…I just know how I feel. In one of your emails you said something that truly touched me…

> "…physically wandering, which leads to mental wandering…with no restrictions, influences, or pressures. My mind is free to travel any-where…very liberating and inspiring. As my mind travels freely with thoughts, my emotions are touched in all different ways, depending on what flows through my mind as I wander on this trail. And this leads to enlightened spiritual freedoms. Amazing, isn't it?"

That is exactly how I was feeling during/after my Ride, I just couldn't figure it out until almost a year after. You brought that feeling back. THANK YOU! I shared your email with my dad, someone who couldn't understand what I was mentally thinking about while riding for 10-13 hours a day. Since that email your sister sent me in May, I have been forwarding them all to him. You are not only inspiring those you already know. Although it's not too clear, my relationship with my dad (always great) has grown, he is learning from me and I believe you helped me with that. You are an amazing writer with an unexplainable experience (at least in my eyes)."

—*Monica Sterk (Tuesday, August 13, 2002)*

"Jarrett, you're absolutely amazing! I think of you, I write to you (in my journal), and you write back. You tell me what I want to hear from you, you tell me words that make me cry, bring a smile from my belly welling up and spilling out of my mouth. How do you do it, pouring words like water down my back, wetting my whole body and cleaning and clearing my conscience, so I can hear, see, feel you inside my heart. Your sensitivity inspires me absolutely. You say things I can't believe, yet I know to be true, but never knew how to express. You've expressed it. In front of a computer no less."

—*Sandra Turshman (Monday, September 9, 2002)*

"I have read every one of your [Jarrett's] emails and Jackie's emails throughout your hike. I have read them, re-read them and forwarded them to friends and family that I thought might appreciate them. I cannot believe it's over, but I can believe you did it. You have more courage that most people I know, and your ability to act upon your dreams and to enjoy life in its most basic form is both admirable and inspirational. Thank you so much for taking the time to send these emails. They have all been great."

—*Nicole Mollen (Tuesday, September 24, 2002)*

"I can only imagine the depth of your hike. The things you saw, the people you met and the feelings and emotions you had/have. Thanks to Jackie, many times I felt I was there. I followed your trip every step of the way, excited to get the next e-mail. It doesn't seem that long ago when we were wishing you well on your journey. Then to receive a postcard from you, remembering something I said once (a lifetime ago) really floored me. After all you have been through and the awesome experience you had, you still had a thought of me. I am honored. I hope we will cross paths again sometime soon, we will both be who we were, we will both be different. Peace."   —*Alan Russo (Tuesday, October 8, 2002)*

—**Thank you friends and family**—

Because of you,
I have been motivated to write the following emails.
And because of your replies,
I have been inspired to write the following book.

*"Thank you all for this motivation and inspiration.
And thank you all for being a part of the journey."*

In peace and love—Jarrett

WALKING WITH PACENCE

—*A True Journey*—

Jarrett Krentzel

iUniverse, Inc.
New York Lincoln Shanghai

WALKING WITH PACENCE
—A True Journey—

iUniverse books may be ordered through booksellers or by contacting:

iUniverse
2021 Pine Lake Road, Suite 100
Lincoln, NE 68512
www.iuniverse.com
1-800-Authors (1-800-288-4677)

ISBN: 978-0-595-39547-7 (pbk)
ISBN: 978-0-595-83944-5 (ebk)

Printed in the United States of America

—Photographs—
Jarrett Krentzel · *Front & Back Cover, Interior*
Sedentary Steve · *Attachment: Pacence (July 14)*
Sedentary Steve · *Author Bio*

—Emails—
Jarrett Krentzel
Jackie
Pacence

—Interview—
Sedentary Steve

—Quotes—
The Appalachian Trail Conference T-Shirt
The Appalachian Trail Companion
Harold Allen
D.H. Lawrence
Cat Stevens · *Father and Son*
Anaïs Nin
Joni Mitchell · *California*
Simon and Garfunkel · *The 59th Street Bridge Song (Feelin' Groovy)*

—Signs—
The Appalachian Trail · *Amicalola Falls State Park*
Leave No Trace · *Seven Principles*
Appalachian Trail Approach · *Amicalola Falls State Park*
Appalachian National Scenic Trail · *Springer Mountain Terminus*
Appalachian Trail · *National Park Service, U.S. Department of the Interior*
Appalachian Trail Halfway Point
The Northern Peaks of the Presidential Range · *White Mountains*
Caution · *100-Mile Wilderness*
Baxter State Park · *Baxter State Park*
Mount Katahdin · *Baxter State Park*
Katahdin · *Baxter State Park*

—Newspapers/Newsletters—
©2002 Newsday, Inc. Reprinted with permission · *Caryn Eve Murray*
Pathways · *Jarrett 'Pacence' Krentzel*

—For Jackie—
I could have only written this book with your help.
"You are a true brother's sister.
I love you."

—Mom & Dad—
Thank you for giving me the experience of a lifetime.
"Your unconditional love has been the greatest gift I know.
I love you both."

—And to all of my friends—
I would have only written these emails with you in my life.
"Your genuine friendship has made me the friend I am today.
I love you all."

—**Thank you Matt**—

Thank you for helping me get started with this book.

"You'll always be 20-pounds lighter in here!"

—Before We Begin—

I've been writing this book for almost two years now. What a journey it has been!

Back in September of 2005, I drove my '78 Volkswagen bus up to Montreal and made my way across Canada with a brand new laptop, a copy of all my journal entries and a printout of every single email message I had once written to all of my friends and family throughout my travels. My original intention for writing this book was to offer something back to my friends and family as a thank you gift for supporting me while I was on my journey and for receiving all of the email messages I had sent along the way.

What you're about to read is a true story. It's an honest experience. And it's an experience that really happened. Nothing in here is false. Nothing is glorified or exaggerated. Everything in here actually took place.

This is a story about peace. And it's a story about love. But mostly, this is a story about truth. A truth that I had once discovered. A truth that I had once experienced. And a truth that I had once lived.

This book has been through many transitions until it was finally ready to be submitted—and let me tell you, it has been quite a process. I have been writing, editing, rewriting, re-editing, re-rewriting, and re-re-editing for the past 'almost' two years now. And in that time, I've tried so hard to find the exact words to express the true feelings I had once felt while I was experiencing my journey. But after many months of trying to get in touch with those words, I eventually realized that the words I've been looking for have already been written...they've been written by me...while I was expressing the feeling!

So in bringing it back full-circle, the following words that you are about to read are the same words that I had once written in my journal entries and email messages throughout my travels. And in keeping true to my original intention for writing this book, this is my way of offering something back to all of my friends and family as a thank you gift for supporting me while I was on my journey and for receiving all of the email messages I had sent along the way.

—So this book I dedicate to all my friends and family—
Thank you all for being a part of the journey back then.
And thank you all for being a part of the journey right now.
"I hope that you will all re-enjoy re-experiencing the following words."

—IMAGINE—

Imagine one day
Everything pauses
God reaches down
Touches you
Unpauses you
Lifts you up
And shows you something that
No eye can see
No ear can hear
No nose can smell
No tongue can taste
No hand can touch.

Imagine experiencing something that
Only your *self* can feel.

Now imagine
God places you back down
Reaches back up
Unpauses everything
And resumes life.

What would you say?
What would you think?
What would you write?

WALKING WITH PACENCE

—A True Journey—

Jarrett Krentzel

—*BEFORE THE TRAIL*—

Journal Entry—
March 6, 2001

You find your…your inner strength, when you're completely broken down. When you're fully broken apart, when you're cracked wide open, it is then, and it is there, when your true colors shine, your true intentions, your true feelings, your true emotions, your purest strength…your purest, truest, most real you…the *you* inside you. The *you* that you bury so deeply within your outer self of yourself…your *you* that is so hidden from your society, your friends, family, your loved ones, and even your own self…the *you* that is so boarded up and stored away and protected. The *you* that is so fragile that must be handled with absolute care…the *you* that may never come out in your entire life, or maybe once…maybe for just one shining moment it is finally revealed, and it is then when you feel most alive, most known, most understood, most real.

But it's so hard…so hard to bring *me* out, so hard to come out. Why? Why, why, why? I'm right here…please, take me, hold me, play with me, love me. Don't love the me you see, love the *me* you feel. Feel *me*. Hear *me*. See *me*. Touch *me*. Love *me*! True love…*me* connecting with *you*…the *me* in me loving the *you* in you. Love. That's how you find it. That's where it exists. It's when you've been completely broken down, fully stripped apart, totally exposed, that's where you find your love, your purest, most real emotion…love. The love inside us all.

Come out. Come out and love all. Love yourself. Let yourself be known. Know yourself??? You already do. Just get in touch. Connect your inner self with your outer self. Make one with yourself. Listen to yourself and do. Hear what yourself is telling your outer self to do and go do it. Don't be afraid of yourself. Express yourself. Make one with yourself. Communicate with yourself and start acting. Don't concern yourself whether it's right or wrong. There's no such thing. You made that up. Forget about it. If they don't like it, you've still won. Rather be yourself and disliked than not be yourself and liked…right?

Journal Entry—
March 13, 01

Tio Alberto (the owner of Tio Alberto's Burrito Shop in San Luis Obispo, California) just said to me, "Stop trying to save the world…the world doesn't want to be saved…if you really want to save something, you must save yourself!"

Save yourself by feeling yourself, not thinking about it…feel it. If it feels right—then go for it!

Journal Entry—
March 18, 01

The truth is negative…that's why you're negative. You know the truth.

This AmeriCorps program (a nonprofit corporation for national and community service) is completely corrupt. I can't believe what's going on here. It's supposed to be nonprofit, but they're making a killing on the side—two hundred thousand dollars in fact! Now that may not seem like a lot of money to most corporations, but out here in the little central coastal town of San Luis Obispo, it's a fuckin' lot—and besides, it shouldn't matter how much money is being made, what matters is that this program is making a profit!!!

I can't believe it. I just can't believe what's going on! Those administrative assholes are all acting like they could really give a shit about the environment, but that's just their front—and educating kids, that's their whole façade. Rip down their awning and we'll all see the truth behind their lie. Those assholes could care less about the environment. They don't give a shit about the kids. And they certainly don't care about this community. What a bunch of shit. What a complete bunch of bullshit this all is! It's all about the money—money, money, money—that's all they ever really cared about!

I've always had a growing suspicion about this program ever since I got hired on back in September. Something just never seemed right here, and that's why I got a hold of the program's budget about three months ago and started running my own underground internal investigation on it—three months of going over figures, talking with community partners, making endless phone calls, and even creating my own mock nonprofit AmeriCorps program for the purpose of comparing my true figures with their manipulated ones—and now, after three months of research, it drives me fuckin' crazy to realize how much those assholes were taking advantage of us. They were lying to us from the very beginning—manipulating the entire AmeriCorps program, abusing the whole nonprofit system, taking advantage of the total San Luis Obispo community—and now that's the truth…that's why I'm negative. I know the truth!

Journal Entry—
March 22, 01

WOW! I can't believe where I've just been. I've just been to the darkest, deepest corners of my mind. The roughest, most extreme angles of thought. The holiest of all my thinking. The dark side. The dark side of my brain. The cave. The hole. The space filled with nothing but dark empty lonely space. Blackness. Completely closed. Unrevealed. Untouched. Unmarked. Unexplored. Unexposed. My weakest link. My deadweight.

It was here where I found peace!
—Believe—

—5 MONTHS, 2 WEEKS & 6 DAYS—

later

Journal Entry—
September 11, 2001

Words—what's left to say?

What's left to think?

What's even left to feel anymore?

It's been almost 6 months since I left San Luis Obispo behind—6 long and lonely months. A lot has happened since I left that town and stormed out in a complete rage. Let's see—after I quit the program, I called the AmeriCorps corporate office in Washington, D.C. and spoke with a program official about all of the profit that was being made. Then, he puts together a team of auditors and flies them out to San Luis Obispo to run an audit on the program. Meanwhile, my director quits as soon as she finds this out, and when the auditors finally arrive, not only do they shut down the entire program for a full week, but they rip through all of the filing cabinets, examine every single file, individually interview all of the 20 AmeriCorps members, and collectively meet with the 4 greedy administrative assholes who were supposedly in charge of running an honest program. And now, after seven years of deceitful operation, that corrupt program is no longer in service. How ironic it all is—the motto of AmeriCorps is *'Make a Difference'*—and although I made quite a difference back there by standing up for myself and what I believed in, here I am, 6 months later, and I'm still feeling completely jaded after the whole experience.

That was 6 months ago—6 months—and now here I am, back in New York, back on Long Island, back in Hicksville, back with my folks, and back to teaching environmental education all over again with this other outdoor ed. program called BOCES (Board of Cooperative Educational Services). I've been hired on as an outdoor naturalist where I facilitate team-building activities that promote peace and trust within groups of kids—at least this program is *honest* about their intentions of making a profit.

Honest—what a joke.

What's honest anymore?

I mean really, what's truly honest these days?

Everything in this world is so corrupt—everything—corporations are greedy, nonprofits are deceitful, people are superficial, society is wasteful—and while all these things continue to spin themselves out of control, everyone seems to get abused in the process, and money continues to be the driving force behind it all. Money—that's what it's all about—money, money, money. It's not about respecting each other. It's not about protecting the environment. It's not about saving the earth. It's about making money, generating a profit, consuming possessions, capitalizing dreams, and taking advantage of everything and everyone in your way. It's all so fucked up to me. Everything in this world is so corrupt. So dishonest. So disrespectful. Where's the honor in anything anymore? Where's the value in life these days? Where's the respect in people? There's so much abuse in this world. So much hate. So much evil. Why? What's the point? What's the point of it all? What's the reason behind all this madness? What's the purpose behind all this insanity? Is it really all for power? All for control? All for money? Is making a lousy profit the real reason behind all this nonsense?

I mean really, why did my AmeriCorps program have to lie to me? Why did they have to manipulate the system? Why did they have to take advantage of the community? And please, somebody please tell me, why in the world did two planes just have to fly into the World Trade Center this morning? Why? Why? WHY? What the hell is going on here?

Just this morning I woke up to teach kids how to build peace and trust within a group, and before I could even begin my lesson, the World Trade Center was brought down by wars and lies. What a day to be teaching kids about peace and trust. Maybe if the adults in this world would just stop bringing each other down with their wars and lies, I wouldn't have to spend my time trying to teach kids how to build themselves up with peace and trust.

It's really all so amazing to me—the human race is so incredibly brilliant. We're all so intelligent. For centuries we've been building technological things that have been improving our way of life—thought, tools, language, shelter, fire, tribes, villages, farms, roads, towns, automobiles, cities, planes, televisions, computers, video games, fax machines, satellites, cell phones, navigational systems— we've been building these things for years, why can't we start building peace today? Why? Why can't we? I'd trade in all these years of technology for just one day of peace!

What are we waiting for? What are we *all* waiting for? A profit from the sky? A spiritual leader from the universe? An almighty god from the heavens? Why should we wait for these supernatural beings when we—human beings—can start building a peaceful world right now? I mean really, if a profit was to really come out of the sky, wouldn't it be rewarding to be recognized as a peaceful race rather than ashamed for our abusive one? Or if a spiritual leader was to really come out of the universe, wouldn't it be blissful to be led forward to an enlightened spirit rather than followed back to our darkened selves? And if an almighty god was really to come out of the heavens, wouldn't it be holy to be blessed for a communal love rather than desecrated for our divided hate?

Why haven't we learned by now? Why haven't we put an end to our madness already? Why do we continue falling down this spiraling mess that we've all created? Why? What's it going take to stop this madness? What's it going to take to end this insanity? What's it going to take to finish this war? More deaths? More destruction? More violence? Do we really need that? Do we really need more planes crashing into buildings? More people jumping for their lives? More buildings crumbling to the ground? Do we really need another day like today to finally realize that we all have to stop this madness before it really gets out of our control?

I mean really, wasn't today enough? Wasn't today enough for our eyes to see? Our ears to hear? Our hearts to feel? Wasn't today enough for our entire world to finally realize that we all have to start building peace right now? Wasn't it? Or was it not? Was it not enough hate? Not enough violence? Not enough war? Was it not enough war for the world to see that putting down our arms and lifting up our embrace is the real solution to our problems?

It's all so crazy to me—building peace is so easy. It's as easy as believing it's possible—and it is possible! It's possible because we *all* still have a chance. We still have a chance to start building peace right now! We still have a chance to start coming together right here! We still have a chance to start gathering as one today! And we still have this chance is because we *all* still have a choice—it's either love or hate, good or evil, peace or war. So tell me—why choose war? Why choose evil? Why choose hate? Why not choose peace, love, and the goodness for all? Why should we continue choosing a hateful race when we can all start choosing a loving one? Why should we continue choosing an evil existence when we can all start choosing a good one? And please, somebody please tell me, why on earth should we continue choosing a warring world when we can all start choosing a peaceful one?

Building peace is all about choice, and each and every one of us has this choice each and every day of our lives—so why not start choosing peace today? It's so easy. It all begins with a simple apology—a simple genuine apology to all—all humans, all animals, all plants, all soil, all water, all air, all life on earth! And it can all end with an easy forgiveness—an easy collective forgiveness from every thing—every life, every creature, every being, every person, every ONE! It's that easy. It's that simple. We can *all* do this. We can all do this together. We just all have to believe—believe it's possible—and it is possible! The choice is ours—it's either start building a peaceful earth today, or continue destroying our abusive world tomorrow.

So…what's it gonna be?

What will we choose?

What will we decide?

What will we all live with tomorrow?

Journal Entry—
December 22, 2001
   —Winter Solstice—
   Just watched *Harold and Maude* with my folks. Brought some sample of reality back into my world.

Reality/my world—what's it all mean???

Reality is outside. My world is inside. I need to connect the two. I need a drastic change.

Right now I live inside—inside a world of walls—inside a world of cars and buses, houses and buildings, shopping centers and strip malls, office complexes and department stores. I live inside a world that's completely surrounded by walls. Walls that aren't real to me. Walls that are fake. Walls that are artificial, unnatural, and made by humans. These walls don't grow. These walls don't breathe. These walls don't touch, or feel, or love. They just divide. They divide and conquer, isolate and segregate, waste away and pollute—and that's exactly what I'm learning from these walls. I'm learning how to waste away and pollute the environment. I'm learning how isolate and segregate myself from others. I'm learning how to divide and conquer the human race. But most of all, I'm learning how to build up my own walls—physical walls, mental walls, emotional walls, spiritual walls—and I'm beginning to feel completely surrounded by them all. I feel trapped, and I can't take it anymore. I want out! I want outside of these walls!

Everything inside here is so unreal to me—everything—TVs and beds, closets and dressers, microwaves and refrigerators, windows and doors—it's all so unreal, all so unnatural—all of it, everything in this society—religion and government, rules and laws, school and work, science and time—it's all been made-up, made-up by humans—humans who have built their unnatural world on top of a natural earth, humans who have poured their synthetic concrete on top of an organic ground, humans who have developed their superficial layer on top of a living skin—and these humans are all acting like this superficial layer is really the earth's genuine appearance, but that's just their front—and all this concrete, that's their whole façade. Rip up the concrete and we'll all see the earth beneath this world!

The earth beneath this world—

That's what I want to see! That's what I want to touch. That's what I want to feel. I want to feel the earth that lives beneath this world. I want to touch the ground that grows beneath this concrete. I want to see the land that breathes beneath this pavement. I want to live with an earth that's living, growing and breathing—not within a world that's dying, sprawling and suffocating. I want to live with an earth that's free and wild and natural—not within a world that's restricted and tame and synthetic. I want to be as free and as wild as the land and the sea—not limited and confined like the walls of this world. I want to be as real and as natural as the plants and the animals—not fake and superficial like the people of this society. But most of all, I want to be as enlightened and as evolved as the touch of nature—not darkened and restrained like the hand of humans.

I can't live inside this world anymore. I can't live inside a world that I no longer believe in—all this unnatural development, all this artificial technology, all this 'so-called' progress, and wasteful pollution, and exploited capitalization—I just don't get it. I don't get any of it anymore! What's the point? What's the point of it all? What's the purpose for all this development, all this technology, all this progress? We don't need any of it. The earth provides us with everything we need to survive with—air, water, food and shelter—so why do we produce all these unnecessary things when our essential needs are already being met, and more importantly, why do we consume all these artificial things when our excessive wants are never fully satisfied? What are we really looking for? What are we really searching for? What do we really want? What are we really missing in our lives?

The human race is clearly suffering from some massive delusional state of physical, mental, emotional and spiritual dissatisfaction, and yet we all still continue to delude ourselves with the constant consumption of meaningless possessions— why? Never do we reach a point where we ever feel completely satisfied with all of our belongings, so why do we continue to consume more stuff, acquire more goods, obtain more possessions, buy more things? The more we buy into these things, the more things we end up buying. It's a vicious cycle of endless consumption that never seems to fully satisfy us—so why do we do it, and more importantly, why do we do it at the expense of the earth's health? The earth is clearly suffering from our wasteful consumption, and yet we all still continue to consume the land in a wasteful manner—why? What's wrong with us? Why do we waste a land that we all need? Why do we pollute an environment that we all use? And most of all, why in the world do we destroy an earth that we all come from?

What is our problem?

Are we really that disrespectful? That insensitive? That greedy? I mean really, what's our desperate reason for destroying an earth that's providing us with life? What's more important than that—our personal level of satisfaction? Is that really more important than the well-being of this planet? The earth is under the weather right now, and if we continue feeding its storm with our toxic production, there'll be nothing left in this world to satisfy us anymore—so what in the world are we doing, and more importantly, what in the world are we all so unsatisfied with? Why can't we just be happy with what we already have? What more do we really need? We've got fax machines, video games, DVD players, digital cameras, cell phones, email addresses, the World Wide Web, Hummers—why can't we just sit back, relax and enjoy it all? Why are we all so obsessed with constantly thinking of more inventions, patenting more ideas, inventing more stuff, producing more things, and consuming more possessions—possessions that aren't even real, possessions that are fake, possessions that are unnatural, harmful and disrespectful to the environment? It's all so messed up to me! Our constant consumption of wasteful possessions is completely out of control, and I just can't support it anymore! I can't support a world that doesn't respect the environment it lives with. I can't support a world that doesn't respect the air it breathes with, or the water it drinks with, or the food it eats with. But most of all, I just can't seem to support a world that doesn't respect the lessons it teaches with.

This world may teach love, it may preach peace, and it may lecture on the truth, but the only lessons I ever seem to be learning in this world are how to hate, how to lie, and how to war—and truthfully, I've got nothing left to learn from a world that teaches its people how to war. I'm not interested in learning from a warring world anymore—I'm interested in learning from a peaceful earth. I don't want to learn from a world that exemplifies lies and hate—I want to learn from an earth that embodies truth and love. I don't want to attend the corrupt institution of this world any longer—I want to start applying myself to the honest foundation of this earth—and the best part of applying oneself to the earth's honest foundation is that we're all immediately accepted—all of us! The earth doesn't reject anyone. It simply accepts us all—and that's the true nature of this earth! *Nature is the earth's unconditional acceptance*, and that's exactly what I want to start learning from. I want to start learning from the earth's nature. I want the earth to be my teacher. I want the earth as my guide!

Right now the earth lives outside—outside with a reality of nature—outside with a reality of plants and animals, rivers and lakes, hills and mountains, moons and stars. The earth lives outside with a reality that's completely embraced by this nature. It's a nature that's real to me. A nature that's pure. A nature that's genuine, natural, and made by itself. This nature doesn't manipulate. This nature doesn't take advantage. This nature doesn't lie, or cheat, or steal. It just unites. It unites and gathers, embraces and connects, supports and cleanses—and that's exactly what I want to start learning from this nature. I want to start learning how to support and cleanse the environment. I want to start learning how to embrace and connect myself to others. I want to start learning how to unite and gather the human race. But most of all, I want to start learning how to get in touch with my own nature—a spiritual nature—and I want to start feeling completely opened by it all. I want to feel released by it, and I want to know that I can accept it evermore. I want in! I want inside of this nature!

Nature—

Nature is outside. I am inside. This is what I need to connect. This is the drastic change that I need. I need to connect my inside self with this outside nature. I need to make one with them. I need to make them whole. I need to get myself outside—outside with the trees, outside with the wind, outside with the sun—and I've got to get myself out of here—out of this world, out of this society, out of these walls! The more I stare at these walls, the more I see them for what they truly are—the real cause of the world's problems, the real cause of the world's divisions, the real cause of the world's disconnections!

Originally, these walls were built to shelter us from an outside nature—rain, wind, snow and heat—but in time, these physical walls have taught us how to build mental walls, emotional walls and spiritual walls to protect us from an inside fear—race, religion, gender and nationality. Eventually, these inner fears were spread out to warn us about an outer appearance—black, white, brown and yellow—and finally, these external appearances were named to divide us from a superficial label—Negro, Caucasian, Mexican and Asian. However, in the end, all these labels are just as made-up as the artificial walls we've managed to surround ourselves with, and while we all continue to relate ourselves to the label—and not the person—we end up establishing a false sense of relationship, because true relationships aren't found within a label, they're found within a being—the human being—and that's the one label we should all be relating to! But we don't. And why? Because we've completely disconnected ourselves based upon the superficial labels we've assigned, the inner fears we've spread, and the artificial walls we've built.

It's all so crazy to me, everything in this world is completely out of control—everything—the artificial walls, the inner fears, the superficial labels, the warring world, the level of dissatisfaction, the excessive wants, the obsessive needs, the mindless consumption, the wasteful possessions, the harmful production, the unnatural development, and the entire disconnected human race—it's all so totally out of hand—and I just don't believe in any of it anymore. I've lost total faith in everything—in the entire system, in the whole program, in the complete façade—and to be perfectly honest, I'm completely embarrassed by this human race and totally ashamed to be a part of humanity. Humanity??? What's so humane about it? Humans the most brutal force on this earth. They're the most insensitive creatures on the planet—and so as far as I'm concerned, humans do not fit my impression of humanity—in fact, they're the most inhumane beings I know—and I can honestly say that I've lost all hope for their entire race!

Wow—I can't believe these words are really coming out of me. I can't believe these thoughts are actually inside my head! I used to be such a peaceful person—so passive, so caring, so loving—but now, now I'm totally skeptical of everything, completely cynical of everyone, and entirely jaded by my experiences—my goddamn experiences with that fuckin' AmeriCorps program! That's when all this disbelief began, and I just can't seem to let go of what happened to me back there in San Luis Obispo. That experience plays over and over again in my mind like a broken nightmare—haunting me in my sleep, keeping me up late at night, leaving me depressed all throughout the day. I have no idea how I'm ever going to get over this one.

I just can't seem to stop thinking about how it all started. It all began way back at the beginning of the program when we were all told that we had to wear these ridiculous uniforms—we all looked like forest park rangers—long sleeve button-down khaki shirts, AmeriCorps patches on both sleeves, brown Dickie pants, steel-toe boots, hard-hat helmets—we were only trying to teach kids about the environment, but for some odd reason the administrative staff had us all uniformed up like we were about to fight the environmental war or something. I never quite understood their logic behind this, but they definitely had their creative reasons, so we all felt obligated to uniform ourselves up with their apparent image. Anyway, I was hired on as the program's team-leader—after already completing a year of service with AmeriCorps up in Portland, Oregon—so along with teaching environmental education to the kids, I was also responsible for attending bi-weekly meetings with the administrative staff. When I first attended these meetings, I was always ready to start discussing the issues that directly related to the development of our program—issues like implementing meaningful community service projects, creating inspiring incentives for youth volunteers, encouraging community member participation—but all they ever wanted to talk about was money—money, money, money! Now I know that it takes money to run any program in this world—nonprofit or not—but what they didn't realize was that I also knew what it took to run an AmeriCorps program in this country.

The AmeriCorps program is a national corporation that helps fund nonprofit organizations all over America. The program operates on a year-to-year basis where the national government grants annual money to organizations for one full year of service. In order to receive this money, a nonprofit organization must first collect half of their budget expenditures through community donations—this proves to the government that there's a definite need for their services within their community. Once this need has been proven, the government will then match this donation by granting the organization the other half of their budget expenditures—in which completely satisfies the organization's annual budget—so it's expected that in any given year, every operating organization has already received all of their annual funds for completing one full year of service, and if they choose to continue servicing their community for an additional year, they must restart the entire grant writing process by recollecting another half of their annual budget expenditures through community donations—and this is exactly what seemed questionable to me about my program. The administrative staff in my program was constantly talking about clever ways to continue raising money for the current year—not the following one—and so this seemed odd to me because I thought they had already received all of their annual money for completing one full year of service. I used to question them about this matter all the time, but they'd always give me some manipulated answer with tons of fake smiles and lots of phony grins. So after several months of hearing the same line of bullshit, my constant questioning eventually turned into a growing suspicion, and soon enough, that turned into a full underground internal investigation on the program—and after three months of researching the program's budget, I finally discovered the truth behind their lie—$200,000 in profit was in fact being made—and when I found this out, I fuckin' lost my mind!

I marched right into their office, tore that corrupt uniform off my body, stripped right down into my boxer shorts and yelled at them at the top of my lungs, "THIS PROGRAM IS FUCKIN' BULLSHIT! THIS IS MORALLY WRONG! EVERYTHING IN HERE IS COMPLETELY UNETHICAL! I DON'T BELIEVE ANY OF YOU ANYMORE! YOU'RE ALL A BUNCH OF FUCKIN' LIARS!!!"—and on and on I went, yelling at them until I had nothing left to yell—and when I was finally done yelling, I then stormed out of their office, got into my car, rolled down the window, held out two peace signs with both of my hands and continued screaming right at my director's face, "WHOSE SIDE ARE YOU ON? WHOSE SIDE ARE YOU ON ANYWAY!!!"—and then I drove off.

I drove myself right down to the beach, got out of the car, grabbed a bag of leftover bread from the backseat and ended up feeding the seagulls for the rest of that morning—I was still in my boxer shorts—and when I was finally done tossing that last piece of bread out to the seagulls, I got right back into my car, drove straight to my house, called the AmeriCorps corporate office in Washington, D.C. and spoke with the program official about all the profit that was being made—and the rest is history—a history that continues to haunt me.

I completely lost it that day—I totally lost my mind back there—and now here I am, still in New York, still on Long Island, still in Hicksville, still with my folks, and still teaching kids how to build peace and trust within a group—and with all that's going on in the world these days with the *War on Terror*, I just can't seem to find any peace in anything I'm doing anymore. I'm trying so hard to make sense of this reality we all live in, but I just can't seem to get a grip on it anymore. All I keep hearing is, "*'United We Stand', 'United We Stand', 'United We Stand'*"—but I just don't know how to unite myself with something I don't stand for. How am I supposed to stand for a war when I'm sitting down with a group of kids and teaching them about peace? I don't believe in war. I don't believe in standing up for a war. And I certainly don't believe in uniting myself with a world that does.

I believe in peace. I believe in love. And I believe in the truth. And I believe that the truth is that we're all a part of one race—not a divided one. We're all a part of one earth—not a bordered one. And we're all a part of one love—not a disconnected one. I believe that we all come from the same nature. We all belong to the same soul. And that we're all connected to the same spirit—it's a collective spirit—a spirit that enlightens us all—all humans, all animals, all plants, all soil, all water, all air, all moons, all suns and all stars. It's a spirit that bonds us all together, supports us all as one, embraces us all communally, and connects us all equally—and I truly believe that we are all a part of this spiritual union.

I don't believe that we are separate. I don't believe that we are divided. And I certainly do not believe that we are better, higher or grander than any other living being in this universe. I believe that we are all grand. I believe that we are all high. And I believe that we are all great. I don't believe in this hierarchy of life where animals are more superior to plants, but less superior to humans. I believe that we are all the same, we are all equal, and we are all alike—and although we may appear to look different on the outside, we all seem to be experiencing the same thing on the inside—LIFE!

But unfortunately, the world doesn't believe this. The world believes something much more unbelievable. The world believes that we are different, we are separate, and we are unequal—and because of this worldwide belief, I am left here with no other choice but to leave it all behind.

Tio Alberto was right—I've got to stop trying to save the world...the world doesn't want to be saved...if I really want to save something, I've got to go and save myself.

I don't want to be a part of this world anymore. I don't want to be a part of the corruption any longer. I don't want to be a part of anything that deals with buying, or selling, or manipulating, or persuading anyone anymore. I just want to do the most simplest thing known to humankind. I just want to eat. I just want to drink. I just want to breathe, and sleep, and shit. But most of all, I just want to walk. That's it. Nothing more, nothing less. I just want to walk...walk in nature.

I've been thinking about hiking a long-distance trail ever since I left San Luis Obispo behind—and now here's my chance! This spring, I'm gonna walk in nature. This spring...I'm gonna hike the Appalachian Trail!

What am I hoping for? Nothing—everything, and all in between.

Journal Entry—
February 26, 2002

I looked at the world in a way in which I haven't seen it for a long time now. I saw it, the world that is, looking through spiritual eyes. Everything appeared physical, way too physical. Too much physics playing into life—not enough spirits. Where am I? Am I lost, or are they? Or is anyone? Or are we all? It's all so crazy to me, I feel found, but...no, I know I'm found...but I feel lost. My mind is telling me that I am right, I'm truthful, faithful, just, but my heart is so pained. Society makes me feel as if I'm lost, wrong, crazy, depressed. Why do I feel this? I know the truth...my truth—why can't I be happy knowing my truth—what's all this pressure about to live another's truth? I want to live my truth, my thoughts, my feelings, my wants, my desires, my wishes, goals, pleasures, my happiness, my truth.

But my truth feels so lonely here...which makes me feel lonely. What is it then? Am I not happy with my truth, or can my truth just not coexist with this society—which makes me feel unhappy? There must be something about my truth that I don't feel entirely confident about...therefore, I must not feel entirely confident about me...I lost confidence in myself...and why? Because others don't agree with me, don't believe in me, don't understand me? Well, I can't worry about that, or them, any longer. It's time to move, time to shift, time to achieve something higher...higher movement, higher shifting, higher thought. I need to focus on my truth and make it true for me. I need to align myself again.

Feelings—thoughts.

Heart—mind.

It's time to align.

—THE TRAIL—

THE
APPALACHIAN TRAIL

MAINE TO GEORGIA

A Footpath for Those Who Seek Fellowship
With the Wilderness

——— • ———

*The Appalachian Trail was conceived
as a way for individuals,
by their own unaided efforts,
to explore the nature
of the major mountain environments of the East
and retreat for awhile
from daily industrialized life.*

From:	Jarrett Krentzel
To:	Friends & Family
Subject:	The Appalachian Trail
Date:	Sunday, March 31, 2002, 7:58pm
Attachment:	Mail Drops.doc

Hello family and friends, brothers and sisters,

I am about to embark on what I hope to be the most inspiring journey of my life; The Appalachian Trail, Georgia to Maine, 2,160-miles, 5-7 months. Hundreds of people attempt a thru-hike (hiking an entire trail in one continuous hike) for many different reasons, and so do I. We walk with many expectations and different levels of success, and we all walk with many hopes and many dreams—or for some, realities. However, the one commonality that we all walk with has become, and is the most important to me—we all walk together, together as a community, a community of thru-hikers. I don't know where my journey will take me, I don't know what my journey will take me through, nor do I know how my journey will fulfill me. All I do know is that I'm starting a hike with the hopes to learn life's most simplest, yet what seems to be life's most complex lessons.

Jackie, my loving sister and right hand hiker, will be my main contact person. I will mostly be in touch with her, where she will then send out these mass emails to keep you all updated on my experiences and progress. If you are interested in following my journey using a detailed poster-size map, here's the information to receive a copy:

Contact The Appalachian Trail Conference (a volunteer-based, private, nonprofit organization dedicated to the preservation and management of the Appalachian Trail) at (304) 535-6331, and ask for the 4-foot Appalachian Trail map. You are allowed to use my member ID# (58133) for a discounted price of $2-3.

If you are planning to meet me on the trail for a day, week, or month, please contact my sister so she can give me a heads up, and if you want to send me anything along the way, I've included an attachment to this email that lists all of the mail drop (a method of re-supply while hiking) information. If you're interested in reading some inspiring literature about the trail, here's a wonderful book to start off with that not only held my interest, but left me with a desire to read more about the Appalachian Trail: *A Walk in the Woods*, by Bill Bryson.

Thank you for all your support this past year. Thank you for both believing in me and understanding me.

Harmony—Jarrett—Love

Attachment: **Mail Drop.doc**

—SPRINGER MOUNTAIN TERMINUS—
(THIS IS MY STARTING POINT 4/15/02)

Mail Drop Address	E.T.A.	Miles to Next Drop	Days to Hike
Walasi-Yi Center	April 18	131	8-9
9710 Gainesville Hwy.			
Blairsville, GA 30512			
Fontana Dam, NC, P.O. 28733	April 26	108.8	7-9
Hot Springs, NC, P.O. 28743	May 3	114	6-8
Roan Mountain, TN, P.O. 37687	May 10	70.2	5-6
Damascus, VA, P.O. 24236	May 15	162.3	11-14
Pearisburg, VA, P.O. 24134	May 26	93	6-8
Troutville, VA, P.O. 24175	June 1	131.2	9-11
Waynesboro, VA, P.O. 22980	June 10	107	7-9
Front Royal, VA, P.O. 22630	June 17	53.7	4-5
Harpers Ferry, VA, P.O. 25425	June 21	123.7	8-10
Duncannon, PA, P.O. 17020	June 29	69.9	5-6
Port Clinton, PA, P.O. 19549	July 4	76.3	5-7
Delaware Water Gap, PA, P.O. 18327	July 9	109.4	6-8
Bear Mountain, NY, P.O. 10911	July 15	64.5	4-5
Kent, CT, P.O. 06757	July 19	112.2	7-9
Cheshire, MA, P.O. 01225	July 26	72.5	5-6
Manchester Center, VT, P.O. 05255	July 31	94.8	6-8
Hanover, NH, P.O. 03755	August 6	69.2	5-6
North Woodstock, NH, P.O. 03262	August 11	74.8	6-8
Gorham, NH, P.O. 03581	August 17	110.1	8-11
Stratton, ME, P.O. 04982	August 25	70	5-7
Monson, ME, P.O. 04464	August 30	*117.8	12-14

*(includes return to Millinosket, ME)

—MOUNT KATAHDIN TERMINUS—
(THIS IS MY ENDING POINT (E.T.A.) 9/12/02)

—MAILING INFORMATION—

Please include:
- My name
- General Delivery
- Mail Drop Address
- Hold for A.T. Hiker
- E.T.A.

(Example for 2nd Mail Drop)

Jarrett Krentzel
General Delivery
Fontana Dam, NC, P.O. 28733

Please Hold for A.T. Hiker
E.T.A.—April 26, 2002

Leaving Hicksville, Long Island, New York

From:	Jackie
To:	Friends & Family
Subject:	The time has come
Date:	Saturday, April 13, 2002, 10:10am

Hello everyone,

This is Jackie, Jarrett's sister. Yesterday Jarrett sent me the first email message that he wanted me to pass along to all of you. He called me today as he had just arrived in Washington, D.C. Bari (his girlfriend) drove him down there—Bari you freakin' ROCK!!!!! As soon as I hear from him again, I'll let you all in on the news. Have a great day and enjoy the following email from Jarrett......

The time has come...I've been thinking about, talking about, and planning this hike for a little over a year now. I've been waiting for this day to come, patiently. And now here I sit, the night before my departure, a whole year later.

I'm not excited, nor am I nervous. I'm just ready.

Send some thoughts, some prayers and some blessing my way...for my time has finally come.

Harmony—Jarrett

Journal Entry—
April 14, 2002

Just left the Greyhound D.C. terminal. How do I feel? There are no words. Can't seem to explain this one. All I can honestly say is that I've never felt such intensity before.

Bari…you're the best. Bari, you are the best. That's all I could say to myself as I waved goodbye to her through the window of my bus. That's all I could say because that's what she is. Bari really was the best to me. She helped me through so much this past year. She was so supportive, so understanding, and so incredibly loving. I'm so thankful to have met her. So grateful to have loved her. But I'm not sorry to be leaving her. I never wanted to leave Bari behind, I only wanted to leave the world.

Thank you for teaching me my first lesson with you…
                    If you believe it, then it's true.
I believe in you, and you are true to me.
It's 8:30pm.

Journal Entry—
April 15

Just pulled into Charlotte, North Carolina for a transfer. It's 4:50am. Walking into that bus station really put into perspective how delirious I feel. All those waiting faces looking back at us (Trevor, Greg and I). Trevor and Greg are two hikers that also boarded the bus back in D.C. They're riding down to Georgia as well to hike the trail. It was real easy to spot them out—big backpacks, broken-in hiking boots, brightly colored bandanas. I've got the same thing going on with me—a huge backpack of my own, hiking boots that I've been breaking in for the past year, and a brand new yellow bandana that's cinched tightly around my forehead. It's comforting to know that I've already met some hikers down here. It doesn't make this solo-journey feel so solo right now.

Well, back on the bus—last leg down to Gainesville—back in my element and feelin' great. The sky is staring to lighten up on the horizon. Should catch a nice sunrise soon. Here we go.

Journal Entry—
April 15, 12:03pm

Amicalola State Park—I'm finally here! Calming energy. A relief. Feelin' great, strong and proud.

As soon as Trevor, Greg and I stepped off that bus back in Gainesville, this huge group of anxious taxi drivers immediately bombarded us. They all wanted to take us up to the park, for this is the time of year when hundreds of Appalachian Trail thru-hikers step off the Greyhound in search of a ride. It took us about an hour to get up here, so the fare was pretty expensive, and that's exactly why all those drivers were restlessly waiting to push their way in front of each other to get to us first. I was so tired from the long bus ride that I just couldn't deal with any of them, but standing behind all those pushy men was a peaceful lady leaning up against her cab—and she seemed like someone I could definitely deal with—so I began parting my way across to her, and with Trevor and Greg following close behind, we all tossed our backpacks into her trunk, jumped right into her cab, and started making our way up to the park.

After spending a full hour in her cab and seventy-five bucks on the ride, we finally made it—Amicalola State Park—and as soon as I stepped out, I instantly felt a wave of peaceful energy. I couldn't tell if this peace was coming from within me or from within the park, but no matter where it was coming from, I definitely felt an intense sense of relief.

Right now I'm sitting down in a grassy field and taking it all in, and when I look all around me, I can clearly see that all of the trees have bloomed down here in the park, but they haven't up there in the mountains. Up there in the mountains the trees are still leafless. Up there in the mountains the Appalachian Trail begins. And up there in the mountains is where I'm headed to—up there with a backpack full a gear.

Trevor and Greg are all geared up and ready to start hiking today. At first I felt like I needed to spend the day relaxing in the park and transitioning myself into my new surroundings, but later I thought that I really wanted to begin hiking with them today. It's an 8.8-mile hike up to the top of Springer Mountain (that's the southern terminus of the Appalachian Trail) on a side-trail called the Approach Trail. Then it all starts mañana. Today, just a leisure walk in the woods.

From:	Jackie
To:	Friends & Family
Subject:	Jarrett's first day on the trail
Date:	Monday, April 15, 2002, 2:50pm

Hi everyone,

YES!!!! I finally got a call from Jarrett today and he's psyched. He took a 13½-hour bus ride from Washington, D.C. to Gainesville, Georgia. On the bus he met two guys who are also hiking the AT—Trevor from Pennsylvania, and Greg from Massachusetts. Once they arrived in Gainesville, they all took a cab up to Amicalola State Park—$75.00 cab ride!! When they got to the park, Jarrett weighed his backpack at a whooping 57-pounds—most of this weight is the food he brought along with him and the water he's carrying, but he did tell me that without this food and water, the weight of his pack is still 35-pounds on his back—UHG!!!

Anyway, he just signed in at the visitor's center as an Appalachian Trail thru-hiker and today he's hiking 8.8-miles on the Approach Trail to get to the top of Springer Mountain—that's where the Appalachian Trail begins. The weather down there is gorgeous. The sun is out, the trees are looking happy, and he's freaking walking to MAINE!!!!! Oh, I just went to the post office and mailed him his food for the next two mail drops that he'll be stopping at.

I'll keep in touch—Jackie

THE APPALACHIAN TRAIL

———— • ————

Here begins the approach trail to Springer Mountain, the Southern terminus of the Appalachian Trail, a continuous footpath extending more than 2,000 miles to Mt. Katahdin, Maine. The Appalachian Trail was conceived by Benton MacKaye, forester, philosopher, dreamer, who in 1921 envisioned a footpath along the crest of the Appalachian Mountains. The Trail is maintained by volunteer hiking clubs, the U.S. Forest Service, and the National Park Service, coordinated through the Appalachian Trail Conference.

"Remote for detachment, narrow for chosen company,
winding for leisure, lonely for contemplation,
it beckons not merely north and south, but
upward to the body, mind, and soul of man."

Harold Allen

GEORGIA HISTORICAL MARKER

Amicalola State Park

Greg, me and Trevor at the entrance of the Approach Trail

DAY 1
Journal Entry—
April 15, 8:49pm

Just hiked 7.3-miles on the Approach Trail up to Black Gap Shelter (a shelter is a three-sided lean-to with a sloped roof). Stayin' here with Woodsy, Greg and Brian from Ohio. Brain is a thru-hiker who we met along the way while he was filtering some water in a nearby creek. Woodsy is Trevor's trail-name (a new identity that thru-hikers take on while hiking the trail). He immediately reintroduced himself just as we were about to enter the Approach Trail—he said that it meant 'man of the woods'. I've always read about these trail-names back when I was planning for this hike. I remember reading that these names were assigned to each other along the way, but I don't recall reading anything about thru-hikers naming themselves out here—I guess Woodsy chose to break that mold, and I guess the mold in which we shape ourselves with is the form in which we end up becoming.

Before we entered the Approach Trail, an older man approached us first. I forget his name, but I remember his title. He introduced himself as an Alumni Appalachian Trail Thru-Hiker, and then he handed us each a pack of matches. On the back it read:

Leave No Trace
1—Plan Ahead and Prepare
2—Travel and Camp on Durable Surfaces
3—Dispose of Waste Properly
4—Leave What You Find
5—Minimize Campfire Impacts
6—Respect Wildlife
7—Be Considerate of Other Visitors

He told us to use the matches if we needed to, but carry the pack out when we're done. He said to carry it out to the first road crossing—a crossing that'll mark a point on the trail known as Neels Gap—and that's where we'll find an outfitters store called the Walasi-Yi Center (my first mail drop in Blairsville, Georgia). He said that if we bring the pack of matches into that store, they'll exchange it for a collapsible plastic water bottle that's been donated by the Leave No Trace organization.

He then told us some statistics about the trail. He said that about 3,000 people attempt to thru-hike this trail each and every year, and only about 300 of them actually make it to the end. I was really surprised to hear that. I figured that a bunch of thru-hikers would dropout along the way, but ninety percent of them seemed like an awful lot. He explained that most thru-hikers dropout within the first 50-miles of the trail because they find that it's just way too difficult for them. After that, several more dropout 250-miles up north in a little town called Hot

Springs, North Carolina because they find themselves getting sucked into all the pleasurable temptations up there—delicious restaurants, comfortable motels, hot showers. He said that Hot Springs is considered to be the first vortex-town of the trail (a vortex-town is a trail-town that entices thru-hikers to stay longer than expected). Beyond Hot Springs, he then warned us about a restless condition up in Virginia where thru-hikers usually get incredibly depressed and end up dropping out all throughout the state. Virginia is the longest state on the Appalachian Trail (550-miles long), and thru-hikers often feel like that state goes on forever and never ends, and they typically find themselves suffering from what it is commonly known as 'The Virginia Blues'—however, he did assure us that if we make it through that state and cross into Harpers Ferry, West Virginia (that's where the Appalachian Trail Conference National Headquarters is located), then as long as we don't break any bones, run out of all our money, or do anything stupid out here, then we're all guaranteed to make it to the end of the trail and climb our way up Mount Katahdin. But after assuring us of this, he did tell us this one story about a thru-hiker who made it all the way up to Maine, and when she finally got her first glimpse of Katahdin in the distance, she got so excited that she started jumping up and down with her backpack still on her back and ended up breaking her ankle. "Unfortunately," he said, "she did not make it to the end of the trail, but she did make it into the ninetieth percentile of thru-hikers who ended up dropping out last year."

I asked him if he could offer us some advice, and the only thing he said to us was this, "*Hike you own hike!*"—that's it—but then he turned all of his attention over to me, stared deep into my eyes, and continued on by saying, "You look strong to me. You seem ready to thru-hike this trail. I know you'll make it to the other end. I know you'll climb your way up Mount Katahdin."—and after hearing confident words like that, I gave him the tightest hug I knew, thanked him deeply, turned myself towards the Approach Trail and took my very first step up Springer Mountain.

The entrance of the Approach Trail was quite profound. It had this huge towering stone arch that welcomed our arrival. It appeared as if that stone arch was our gateway into the natural world, and I knew that once I had passed through it, there was no turning back—the only way back out is to climb down Mount Katahdin at the other end. To the left of that towering stone arch was a long wooden sign that read:

> APPALACHIAN TRAIL APPROACH
> SPRINGER MTN., GA. 8.5 MILES
> MOUNT KATAHDIN, MAINE 2,108.5 MILES

And now here I am, after climbing 7.3-miles up this Approach Trail, and I'm spending the night here in Black Gap Shelter. I just ate two packages of veggie noodles and several handfuls of trail-mix. Brian showed me how to hang my food bag up in the trees (keeping it out of reach of bears). It's nice to have someone help you out out here. I've never done this before. This is my first time backpacking. Been car camping and day-hiking before, but this my first time putting them both together like this, so I'm a bit out of my comfort zone here. First night—I guess it's expected. Took a piss after dinner—walked into the woods without my headlamp on…it was so dark and cold out there—almost cried. Kept strong. Today was a challenge, but I made it. Tomorrow I head for the top of Springer, and then the AT begins. Have to listen to my body. Listen, respect and work as one with my body.

The Approach Trail

APPALACHIAN
NATIONAL SCENIC TRAIL

SPRINGER MOUNTAIN
ELEVATION 3782'

Southern Terminus

CHATTAHOOCHEE
National Forest

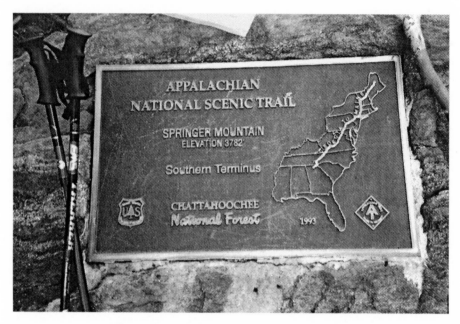

The Southern Terminus of the Appalachian Trail

DAY 2
Journal Entry—
April 16, 10:26am

Springer Mountain terminus—just breathtaking (3,782-feet). Feelin' good. My left knee hurts a bit on the incline. Lots of gnats up here. Woodsy said that he saw a meteor shower last night as well. He just asked us a great question about contemplating this hike. I was really surprised to hear him ask that—I guess he did. Never crossed my mind once, but I did tell them that I almost cried last night. Felt good to admit myself. Keep true—honest to my feelings, body and mind.

Journal Entry—
April 16, 5:54pm

Made it—Black Hawk Shelter. It's beautiful in here. Three stories/levels with nooks and crannies everywhere to store hiking poles/boots/whatever. Met up with some more hikers today—Deacon, who helped me with my penny whistle—he and Radar (Greg's trail-name because someone thought that he looked like the character Radar on the TV show M*A*S*H) helped me get this long piece of cardboard paper (filled with instructional musical notes) out of the whistle. Also met Christina and Eric from Maine. She lent me her knee brace. It's a bit sore. Hope it's nothing major?

Burned some sage and had a ceremony up on Springer Mountain this morning. Felt nice. Smelled great. Knee still hurts a bit, but feeling groovy. Deacon has a radio with him and we heard Billy Joel. He was surprised to hear me sing along. And trail-life begins.

DAY 3
Journal Entry—
April 17, 8:30am

Privy mean outhouse—sat on the privy this morning facing the sun making its way over 'them' hills. Everyone says 'them' out here. It's always 'them hills' or 'them folks'. It's never 'those hills' or 'those people'. I guess that's all a part of being down here in the great south, and you know what, I kind of like it. It really makes me feel like I'm in Georgia. If it weren't for the speech, I'd never know otherwise. The woods are the woods no matter where you go. But the lingo is the language depending on 'where ya is'.

Everyone's talking about gettin' to Neels Gap. Talkin' about sending some weight home—not items—weight. I'm thinking about trading in my backpack—it's just too big and heavy for me—although I am startin' to get a system down with it. I'm sure it will change everyday. Put on my gaiters (a tough outer fabric that protects boots and ankles from low ground brush) this morning. Felt like a real hiker. Peace.

Journal Entry—
April 17, 7:08pm

Trail-magic—it's a hard term to define on paper. It's difficult to find the exact words to explain what it means, or feels like, or how magical it actually makes the trail feel. It comes in all forms, all situations, all the time, as long as you're aware of its occurrence.

Today trail-magic began when Deacon and I took our first break of the day. The ibuprofen was wearing off and man, my knee was really starting to act up again. Deacon and I sat down on a huge log together and he started telling me his reasons for thru-hiking the trail. That seems to be a most common conversation right now. If you're not talking about the gear in your pack, you're usually talking about the reasons for your hike. He began by telling me that this is his second attempt to thru-hike the trail. His first attempt was years ago when he started hiking on his own as well. A couple of months into that hike, he finally met up with another thru-hiker that he really connected with, an older man much like himself—he called this man a trail-friend. He said that they were absolutely inseparable together, hiking mile-after-mile and day-after-day with each other, but by the time they made it up to Connecticut, his trail-friend got such a bad infection on his foot that he was forced to leave the trail behind. Deacon said that one day they had to climb over this tall wooden fence and his friend just couldn't make it over on his own—and that's when his friend knew that it was time for him to leave—so he stuck his hand out through a small opening of the fence and shook Deacon's hand goodbye. That was a real sad day for the both of them, however Deacon continued on by himself, but after walking with such a great trail-friend for so long, Deacon soon found himself getting more and more depressed because it was really hard for him to continue hiking on his own—so he eventually left the trail behind as well. Deacon has always kept in touch with his trail-friend through the years, but just recently he found out that his friend had passed away—and that's exactly why he's out here for a second attempt—Deacon's thru-hiking the Appalachian Trail in memory of his trail-friend.

I was so touched by his reason for being out here—and after listening to him for about an hour or so, we just continued sitting there on that log in total silence—and that's exactly when a little taste of trail-magic flew right passed us. I mean literally flew. It soared about 12-feet from us and just about eye-level. It shot both Deacon and I right up to our feet. It flew right by us and took its rest in a nearby tree. Well, that was enough for Deacon and I to grab our packs and continue on. I can't say for sure how or why my knee felt so good after standing up, but I can definitely say that that hawk sure did sprinkle some trail-magic our way.

Call it what you want, and even call it, or me, crazy, but something magical happened out there for me. Something magical sure did occur out there. And that wasn't the end of a truly magical day.

As we continued making our way down the mountain, we suddenly found ourselves surrounded by an entire army of troops. Everywhere we looked, we were surrounded by big green men. They were everywhere. It was as if we were under attack. But we weren't. No one was—yet. These big green men weren't attacking anyone at the present moment, but rather they were all in training for a future attack—and there were hundreds of them out there, maybe thousands of them—and they were all uniformed up in head-to-toe army gear.

There we were—leisurely making our way down the Appalachian Trail, hiking at our own freedom, holding onto our lightweight hiking poles and wearing our comfortable hiking shorts and polyester T-shirts that supposedly wicked sweat away from our bodies—and there they were—busting their asses up the entire face of that mountain, being whistled at by their commanders, gripping onto their oversized machine guns and bearing the weight of their heavy-duty jackets, canvass pants, steel-toe boots and hard metal helmets that were all tightly strapped around their sweaty shaven heads.

Deacon and I just stopped in our tracks and looked over at each other with blank faces. We didn't know what to say, so we just paused there and stood still while this entire army of human weapons busted their way up to the Appalachian Trail and over that mountaintop. It was like we were watching an entire herd of controlled animals. I really had no idea what to think, so rather than thinking at all, I just stood there with an empty mind and watched this entire army charge its way all around me. They charged from all directions—from the right, from the left, from down below, from up above—they were everywhere in sight and I felt completely surrounded by them all, and while I felt totally bordered by their charge, they all seemed absolutely oblivious to me, so I just kept standing there in the middle of their stampede until their dust finally cleared and settled to the ground—and when Deacon and I no longer heard their commander's whistle in the distance, without saying a single word to each other, we just slowly continued making our way down the trail.

I finally pushed myself all the way down to the creek—Justus Creek (1-mile from the shelter—Gooch Gap Shelter). I soaked my knee in the creek and filled up my water bottles, and while I was in the creek filtering water, Deacon comes running over to me and says, "You won't believe Iron Horse (another thru-hiker who we met along the way)—a tall, muscular man from Texas—he just jogged a mile back here to help you carry your load!" And that's exactly what happened. I walked behind Iron Horse in my Tevas (sandals) while he carried my backpack for 1-whole mile. He truly is a good soul, 'cause after I was done telling him about my 'making a difference' with AmeriCorps by standing up for myself and for my beliefs, he then responds with, "You're a great man!" Now here's a man who just jogged 1-full mile back to the creek to carry my load and help me out with my bum knee, and he's calling me a great man! Funny how things work out in life. Inspiring how life works out things.

My blessings and prayers to Iron Horse and his girlfriend, who I keep forgetting her trail-name, but I do remember that she's from Canada, and she told me that Trillium is the countries flower. Anyway, I wish them both all the blessings to a truly magical flight to wherever their destination may be—whether that's in their minds, for their bodies, or the spiritual enlightenment of their souls. I wish them both the ease of a flight to that of a hawk.

Iron Horse's girlfriend, Iron Horse, Woodsy, Radar, Deacon, Brian, Olgoat and me
at Gooch Gap Shelter

DAY 4
Journal Entry—
April 18, afternoon
Dream—

Olgoat (a southbound thru-hiker from Maine—2 days left), in my thoughts while asleep. His finger I kept looking at—the nail side—it was held up behind some cardboard blocking. His voice was talking with me. I think I was responding. One thing I remembered was that he kept referring to something as 'COOS'. Whispering it as if it was, or is, this really bad word…a terrible word. He said that it meant, "Ones who believe in evil gods!" I suspect he was warning me of such things out here.

Woke up to a heavy downpour. Awake now with Bill, some other man, and a lady with her dog Sam—all solo-hikers. Everyone else left early this morning—Woodsy, Radar, Brian, Deacon, Iron Horse and his girlfriend all continued north, while Olgoat continued south. I stayed back here to rest up my knee.

'COOS'…can't make any sense of it?

Journal Entry—
April 18, 8:20pm

Second night at Gooch Gap Shelter—knee is feeling a little better. Still taking it easy though. Looked for some inspiring words in Kim's pouch (just before I left for the trail, my friend Kim gave me a small see-through pouch that was filled up with inspirational quotes, incense, beads and other symbolic mementos). Pulled out,

"The human soul needs actual beauty more than bread."—D.H. Lawrence

Today was truly a beautiful day, filled with good souls and plenty of relaxation. Took a shower in the spring today. Something about cleaning yourself in the outdoors, using the resources of the outdoors, that cleans you on so many different levels. Of course physical, but much more spiritual. Filtered water from the spring today and clasped my hands together in gratitude for the earth—"The water flows to clean and drink me." I watched all that flowing water and focused in on one drop—thought about the entire cycle—one drop flows down the spring, into a river, into an ocean, up to the sky, and back down to the earth—one drop flows with all drops—all drops flow together…together as a body…a body of water. I bowed my head down in respect—"We can learn so much from water, for we too are one drop, one drop of life…living together…together as a community…a community of humans."

I didn't eat much today. A lot of walnuts and fruit in the morning and a candy bar and pasta at night. That's about it. I guess after all, my soul needed beauty much more than bread today, but I still think I should wait it out for tomorrow.

We'll see at sunrise. Ah…sunrise. Nothing like it, especially the orchestra of birds that accompany its arrival. Goodnight.

DAY 5
Journal Entry—
April 19, 6:12

This is your journey. This is your journey. *Take your time. Think a lot. Think of everything you've got. For you will still be here tomorrow, but your dreams may not.*

Journal Entry—
April 19, 8:??pm

WEAK IN THE KNEE = FEAR

So what's it all mean? I learned my lesson. *Hike your own hike.* This is my journey. Walk it, or journey it at my own leisure. Okay. I'm going to, but I can't continue feeling like this—my knee that is. Do I rest? Do I continue slowly? Do I rest? Do I continue slowly? I don't know. I need to stay and heal, but I so badly want to get to Neels Gap, call Jackie, mom, dad and Bari, tell them all that I'm doing alright and to rest easy. I hope Mark (a hiker that I met in Gooch Gap Shelter who offered to call Jackie when he gets to Neels Gap and tell her that I'm doing fine, just taking a break while resting up my knee) provides some comfort when he calls on Saturday. I want to change up my gear (at the Walasi-Yi Center), send some weight home, pick up my mail drop, get going, but I don't believe I can make it that far with this bum knee. What should I do? What should I do? I'm asking for everyone's advice, internalizing it, drawing up my own conclusions, but staying here is not what I want…it's what I need! Need vs. want—heart vs. mind. My heart needs to rest my knee. My mind wants to continue on. Listen to my heart. Respect my needs. My wants may take me far, but my needs will take me much further. I think…no, I believe…NO, I know what I'm going to do. Right now, tonight…I'm making the decision to stay…

Let's see what I feel I need I want
tomorrow?

DAY 6
Journal Entry—
April 20, 11:??am

Transitions…there weren't any. I mean leaving Long Island, driving down to D.C. with Bari and catching a Greyhound bus to Gainesville is all a physical state of transition to Amicalola State Park. But there has been no emotional, mental or spiritual transition. Once I reached the park—BANG!—13½ hours on a bus and

I jump right into an 8.8-mile Approach Trail to the top of Springer Mountain. My body was in it, but my heart, mind and soul were not.

I needed to rest that Monday morning in Amicalola. Feel the park. Acquaint myself with my new surroundings. Establish myself. But I didn't. Woodsy and Greg (now Radar) were both really anxious to get going. And Bari suggested that I should start once upon arrival. But me, I, Jarrett knew what I needed. I needed to relax and transition. But I didn't, and look at that…I realize my faults and the clouds break open for the first time today. Sunlight shines down on me with my discovery. Anyway, getting back, I felt the pressure of others, the influence of what was best for others, and the result of all this? The result is that everyone is pushing on, including me, but I in a much different way. Now a wind blows over me. The sun is still shining. The leaves are whistling. Self-discovery. That's what this journey is about…self-discovery…self-discovery of the body, mind, heart and soul. With a bum knee that's slowly healing, I've sacrificed my body to learn what my true intentions are—to discover the inner-self. And I must do so by carrying myself at my own pace, uninfluenced by others, and only influenced by my own heart, mind, body and soul. I regret to listen to myself at first, and now I pay the consequence. A great lesson in life. A great lesson for life.

Pulled out another quote from Kim's pouch. It read:

> What another would have done as well as you,
> do not do it. What another would have said as
> well as you, do not say it, written as well as you,
> do not write it. Be faithful to that which exists
> nowhere but in yourself—and thus make yourself
> indispensable.
>
> —Unknown

Gooch Gap Shelter

Journal Entry—
April 20, afternoon

"COOS"—it was my finger, but it was on him. I was talking to my finger, and my finger was responding in his voice. 'COOS'—one who believes in evil gods! My finger, my finger on my left hand, the pointer one…it had been chewed up by me on the right side of the nail. It wears a band-aid now. But that's not the point. Filtration of abuse…that's the point. I abused my finger because something—people, society, friends, family, myself—abused me at, or on, whatever level…it doesn't matter. It's still abuse. Abuse, or one who abuses, is one who gives into evil, or, or therefore one who abuses is one who believes in the evil gods. "COOS" is one who abuses. To COOS is to abuse. That's why I stop biting, or abusing my fingernails out in nature. Nature doesn't abuse. COOS doesn't exist in here…in nature.

The human soul needs actual beauty more than bread. In here, in nature my soul feeds off beauty. Out there, in society my soul feeds off bread. And when a soul feeds off bread, it feeds from COOS.

Journal Entry—
April 20, dusk

Trail-angel…another concept I've read about, heard of, thought about. Never met one before. Until today. "Nice pack." That's how it all took off. And then he just came right over to me and handed over his Boy-Scout T-shirt as a souvenir. After I commented on his pack, the conversation took off…and off and off it went…and continued on…and on and on and on. First we talked about his pack, then we moved onto gear-talk, he gave me all sorts of suggestions—like finding two sticks in the woods and using them as chopsticks instead of carrying around my fork, knife and spoon, to cleaning out my pot with filtered water and then drinking it when I'm done to conserve natural resources, to not carrying a sponge or soap around with me out here, but rather finding these things in town and then using them out there, to clothes that I should keep, clothes I should send home, different kinds of stoves, knives, sleeping bags, food…everything a hiker needs out here, which ain't much, and he proves it by example. He's got all the light/no gear possible, and that's not because he can afford it—he can't—he comes from a poor family, so he's been forced to teach himself how backpack in the woods using whatever resources are available. For example, instead of using a Therm-A-Rest (a lightweight self-inflatable mattress pad), he'll stuff a plastic garbage bag up with leaves for extra insulation and comfort.

We hung our food bags up together on the bear lines (a permanent cable rigged high between two trees specifically for hanging food out of reach of bears and other critters), talked about family, teachers, society, mentors, life. I was so thankful to have met him that I gave him my Swiss Army knife pack (knife/flashlight/compass/magnifying glass/thermometer). He was stunned, and as good as he felt…well, that's how good I felt. He then gave me a stick that he's been carving to walk with. He knew about my knee. Funny, his ankle is swollen as well, but he's strong and dealing with it quite nicely. Then he approaches me with his knife…and hands it over. Says I'll need this. I was stunned…speechless. I know he felt as good as I did, because we both embraced each other tightly. Made a pact to stay in touch. Whether we do or don't, I can guarantee that we will never forget our time here at Gooch Gap Shelter. I sure know I won't.

Thank you Carey Lewis, 15-years old and wise. I wish you all the success and blessings in life. I hope you carve your life's trail with the blade of your soul, the sharpness of your mind, the handle of your heart, and the cutting strength of your body. Much like the blade, sharpness, handle, and cutting strength of our new knives.

From:	Jackie
To:	Friends & Family
Subject:	Jarrett's doing great
Date:	Sunday, April 21, 2002, 8:22pm

Hi everyone,

I hope you're all having a nice weekend. Today I took a 7-mile walk around the neighborhood and when I came back to my home there was a message on my machine. Unfortunately, it wasn't Jarrett, but a gentleman named Mark Fishon who met Jarrett on the trail. According to the message, Jarrett is doing great. He's been resting up his knee in a shelter since it's been bothering him, but Mark assured me that he's doing just great and having such a wonderful time. I take it that Jarrett is still in Georgia from the message Mark had left. He was scheduled to stop in Blairsville, Georgia on the 18th, and I had assumed that he would've called me if he had arrived, but since I haven't heard form him since last Monday (April 15th), he must still be walking his way there. Once he gets to Blairsville, he'll then be crossing into North Carolina. I've already mailed him his food for his two mail drops in North Carolina.

As always, I will keep you posted. Have a great day!

—Jackie

From:	Jackie
To:	Friends & Family
Subject:	Finally heard from Jarrett
Date:	Monday, April 22, 2002, 4:07pm

Hi everyone,

I'm at work right now and I was so excited when the secretary told me that line-1 was Jarrett. This is what he has told me......

The first day on April 15th he hiked 7.3-miles on the Approach Trail. That night he stayed at Black Gap Shelter. The Approach trail was a killer, very steep, and due to this, he sprained his left knee. The next morning he walked 1.5-miles to the top of Springer Mountain, which is the starting point of the Appalachian Trail. He sat up there with a couple of hikers, said some prayers and had a little ceremony. He then walked 7.6-miles to Hawk Mountain Shelter. His knee was swelled up a bit and it was starting to really bother him. He took an ibuprofen (Jarrett told me that hasn't taken any form of western medicine in the past three years). The next morning he walked 8-miles to Gooch Gap Shelter, this is the newest shelter on the trail. On the way there he took a break and hung out with an older man named Deacon (this is his trail-name). While they were hanging out, a huge hawk flew right passed them at eye-level and about 12-feet away. As they watched this hawk pass on by, Jarrett stood up with total inspiration and noticed that his knee was instantly feeling better. I told him that the ibuprofen was probably kicking back in. Anyway, he finally made it to Justus Creek where he filtered some water, rested his knee and relaxed there for a little while.

On his way to the creek, he met a few people that saw that his knee was bothering him, and so while he was sitting down in Justus Creek, all of a sudden a man comes running up to him and says, "I heard from the other hikers back at the shelter that your knee is hurting you!!" This man, named Iron Horse (this is his trail-name), grabbed Jarrett's backpack and told Jarrett to follow him back to the shelter. This experience is called 'trail-magic'—an experience when people on the trail help out other hikers.

Finally he made it to Gooch Gap Shelter and stayed there for three days to rest up his knee. People left him food, as well as some medicine. He met a doctor along the way who is also hiking the AT, and he gave Jarrett a full medical knee examination on the back of Jarrett's backpack. The doc said that he was just fine, nothing too serious had happened to him, he only sprained his knee and that he should keep off it until it feels better.

On his last night in the shelter, the Boy Scout Troop-103 stayed there and he met a kid, age-15, named Carey Lewis who he became good friends with. This

15-year old boy told Jarrett how he can minimize the weight of his backpack and live simpler on the trail. Jarrett gave him his knife as a thank you gift, and Carey gave him his knife as well.

On the morning of the 21st, Jarrett was finally ready to hike out of the shelter and he said to himself, "Either I'm gonna hike out of here and continue building up my body as a hiker, or I'm gonna hike out of here and continue breaking it down and be forced to leave the trail behind." Well, it looks like he continued on as I hiker, because yesterday he made it out of Gooch Gap Shelter and hiked about 8-miles to the bottom of Big Cedar Mountain where he camped out for the night. When he woke up this morning, the 22nd, it was raining out and he said that it felt great. He made it over Blood Mountain, which is 4,461-feet tall, and back down the other side into Neels Gap, which is in Blairsville, Georgia. That's where he is right now, and that's where he just called me from. He was supposed to be there on the 18th, so he's off schedule by four days.

Wow, this is a great long email. Speak to you all soon. Ciao!

—Jackie

DAY 10

Low Gap Shelter Register (a notebook typically found in shelters that hikers use to write messages for other hikers who will come after them) Entry—
4-24 (morning)

Knee's feeling better. Blister problems though. Nothing major. Nice place to rest last night. Pushin' 15-miles today. Let's see what happens.

Harmony—Jarrett

Journal Entry—
April 24, sunset

14.9-mile day. Whew! First 5-miles steady. Then came the three big mountains ending with Tray (4,430-feet). Incredible views from up top. Let out a big scream of excitement three times. Twice when I thought I was at the top, and once when I actually was. Lots of hikers up here (Tray Mountain Shelter)—Shera, Giggles, Meagan and dog Sammy, Booger, Emily and some others.

When I left Gooch Gap Shelter four days ago, I started walking with these two section-hikers (hikers that attempt to hike an entire trail in a series of connected hikes over a period of time) named Don and Chris. They left the trail this morning, so last night they gave me all of their extra food. After finishing dinner with them, they asked me if I wanted a mini-cup of chocolate pudding for dessert. I licked out the entire cup clean, and after I was done, I asked them for another. They said that I could have as many as I'd like—so after licking out the second cup, I licked out a third, forth and fifth cup clean, and that's when they said to me that I might as well finish off the entire 6-pack. After licking out the 6th and final cup of chocolate pudding, they then asked me why I didn't have a trail-name yet. I didn't know. I guess I was just waiting for the right one to come along. So before they went to sleep, they said that they were going to think about it and give me one in the morning.

When we all woke up this morning, we hiked out to the road crossing where their wives were picking them up. I waited with them for awhile at the trailhead (a point where a trail leaves a road crossing) parking lot, and that's when they told me that they had a trail-name for me. They said that they came up with two names. The first one was kind of a joke. They said that because of all the chocolate pudding I ate last night, they were going to name me Pudding, but after laughing about it for awhile, they said that I didn't look like the kind of guy who'd be called Pudding out here. So they thought about it some more and finally came up with a trail-name that they felt really fits. They said that they started thinking about the kind of person I am, how I handle myself out here, what they've always felt from me, how I've always stopped and listened to them whenever they talked to me, how I spoke to them, how I walk, cook my dinner, and even how I filter my water—they said that I do it all with such patience, and so that's the exact trail-name they came up with for me—Patience.

I was so honored. So touched by their offer. What an amazing gift. I gave them both two really big hugs and thanked them both deeply. They said that their wives might still be awhile and that I didn't have to wait with them any longer, so I thanked them once again, exchanged addresses and phone numbers, hugged them both goodbye, and then turned myself towards the trail. I started walking away from them, and as soon as I left them standing there in that empty parking lot, it was as if I was leaving much more than just Don and Chris behind—it was as if I was leaving a part of myself behind as well. I really can't explain it anymore than that, but it really felt like I was stepping out of myself and into someone else—like I was stepping out of Jarrett Krentzel and walking into Patience. I know it sounds crazy, but that's exactly how it felt, and as I continued feeling this way, I started to think about what my trail-name really means to me…

"To be patient is to be peaceful. To be peaceful is to be at peace with oneself. And to be at peace with myself is to *hike my own hike*, walk my own walk, journey my own journey—*pace my own self*—and to *pace* my own self, is to walk with *PACE*nce!"—and the moment I realized the spelling of my trail-name, that's exactly what I started walking with…I started *Walking With Pacence*.

Just sang *Here Comes the Sun* with She-ra and Giggles. Did Cat Stevens or The Beatles write that?

Walking With Pacence

DAY 11
Plumorchard Gap Shelter Register Entry—
4-25

Met up with some old friends from Gooch Gap Shelter (Iron Horse and his girlfriend, Hattie Mae—that's her trail-name). It's nice to recognize and be recognized.

Sharky and Coral (two thru-hikers that I met along the way): Looks like the sun came out after all.

Meagan (a thru-hiker that I met back at Tray Mountain Shelter): Didn't need to use the 2nd Skin (a gel-like pad that protects blisters and helps reduce pain). Blessings on your (job) interview, Sunday.

Harmony—Jarrett→Pacence

DAY 13
Journal Entry—
April 27, sunset

Met Katu (The Whistler—his trail-name). Originally called The Whistling Jackrabbit because he whistles while he walks fast, but he thought that that name was too long…so now he's just The Whistler, a Japanese author who wrote several books about John Muir, and now he's writing one on the AT. He's section-hiking for the next 2-years, talking with thru-hikers along the way and then writing his book. I'd love to read it, but it will only be published in Japanese. He's the first person I truly connected with out here. We talked about levels and how we both believe in leveling ourselves with all humans/animals/plants/each other. Burned sage today. Gave thanks and played my penny whistle…I knew he was watching, listening, processing, and I was comfortable with that, with him. He asked me if that was part of my religion. I said yes, but only I practice it—something for me to give thanks…thanks for the water, sun, earth, and meeting Katu, The Whistler.

My Tiger-Eye necklace broke (Back in San Luis Obispo, my friend Sandra told me about the different Chakra points, or energy centers in the human body. She said that there are seven points, and if any one of these centers is out of balance, it can lead to physical, emotional or mental disharmony. She said that she had sensed some disharmony in my upper stomach region—a region that's supposedly the seat of all my emotions, giving me a sense of personal power and freedom to be myself. She then told me that all seven Chakras have a healing stone for protection, and the Tiger-Eye stone is the healing stone that protects this upper stomach region. Before I left San Luis Obispo, she said that she was going to make me a Tiger-Eye necklace for protection—but I unexpectedly left town too soon and never received her gift. After I flew back to New York, I met Bari a couple months later, and for my December 13th birthday, she makes me a Tiger-Eye necklace without knowing anything about my experiences out west with Sandra. I've been wearing that Tiger-Eye stone around my neck ever since Bari put it on me, and for the first time on the trail, the necklace broke on its own). It happened right after I took a picture of Katu and I, with my arm extended out holding the camera. I snapped the photo, and then immediately after I felt it drop inside my shirt down to my belly. Meaning? I have to think about it. Goodnight.

DAY 14
Journal Entry—
April 28, afternoon

It was raining, and it was windy, and I was wet and cold. And I was hiking, hiking, hiking…climbing up and down, winds blowing from all directions, rains slapping up on my face…and then finally, there she was, my 5,000-foot challenge of the day. Breathe in, breathe out…climb up and up, wind, rain, cold, wet, climb up and up and up…"I'll look at my Data Book (a guidebook that lists all of the distances between shelter locations, water sources, road crossings, mountain summits and other resourceful information along the trail) when I reach the top," I think to myself as the wind blows rain in my direction. Up and up I climb until finally…"Am I there yet?" I wonder. "Better not count your chickens before they hatch. Don't look at that book just yet. Hike a bit further and then see."—I think to myself as I start to walk down and down and down. And as I walk down, the rain begins to settle, the wind calms to a stillness, the clouds begin to stir, and the sun exposes the light. At this point, I don't care where I am, or where I'm gong to next…I'm already here…peacefulness! I've reached a state of peace after battling the weather and mountains. It was here when I first realized what hiking the AT means—PEACE!

From:	Jackie
To:	Friends & Family
Subject:	Jarrett
Date:	Wednesday, May 1, 2002, 8:42pm

Hi everyone,

I spoke to Jarrett last night. He is finally in Fontana Dam, North Carolina.

April 22nd—He made it to Neels Gap. There was an outdoor gear store there called the Walasi-Yi Center and he spent almost half the day with a salesperson going over things to keep and things send back. When Jarrett started the trail, his backpack weighed 57-pounds. Now it's down to 27-pounds, more or less. That night he stayed at a hostel and the owners made this amazing strawberry kiwi shortcake and shared it with him. Jarrett took his first shower at this hostel—his first one since April 14th.

April 23rd—Jarrett met two guys named Don and Chris who are doing what they call a section-hike. They are not hiking the whole trail, just the first 50-miles of it. They've all been walking together since Gooch Gap Shelter, and on this day they hiked 10.6-miles and stayed at Low Gap Shelter.

April 24th—Don and Chris went home. They live near Harpers Ferry, West Virginia and they offered Jarrett a place to stay and chill when he gets up there. Before they left the trail, they gave Jarrett his trail-name…Patience…but he spells it like this, P-A-C-E-N-C-E. Jarrett walked 14.9-miles from Low Gap Shelter to Tray Mountain Shelter.

April 25th—Jarrett walked 14.9-miles from Tray Mountain Shelter to Plumorchard Gap Shelter.

April 26th—This day he crossed the Georgia-Tennessee line. He walked 12.2-miles from Plumorchard Gap Shelter to Standing Indian Shelter.

April 27th—Jarrett walked a whooping 19.7-miles to Rock Gap Shelter. He hiked over this one mountain called Standing Indian Mountain (5,498-feet), which has been the tallest mountain so far. He met a Japanese man named Katu and his trail-name is The Whistling Jackrabbit. He's an author and writer for Japanese outdoor magazines. He's currently writing a book on the AT and he interviewed Jarrett and took some pictures of him as well.

April 28th—He walked 19.6-miles to Cold Spring Shelter. On this day there was a huge rainstorm. Jarrett walked over 10-miles in this cold, wet storm. He was so determined to get over this one mountain so that he could stop for the day. The mountain he was climbing over was called Wayah Bald Mountain, and it's 5,342-feet tall. After he made it over to the other side, it was so sunny and peaceful there. Jarrett felt so content and happy that he was on his journey. He really couldn't explain what he was feeling, but in so many of my own words—he was like a kid in a candy store.

April 29th—On this day he walked 18.4-miles to Sassafras Gap Shelter. He had to walk through this one town called Wesser, North Carolina, and after walking through the woods for the past 2 weeks, he found that there was just way too much activity going on there for him—a lot of people driving their SUV's, tons of traffic, lots of people walking around town. He felt so overwhelmed seeing all of these people—since he hasn't seen so many people in awhile—however he did stop and have some lunch in town. He ate a garden salad, a gyro (I can't believe it, he hasn't eaten meat in almost two years—he said that hiking in the woods has given him an appetite for eating meat again), four lemonades, a Snickers bar, a bag of Funyuns and two chocolate chip cookies. While he was eating all of this food, an older man approaches him and says, "Jarrett! Is that you?" Well holy shit, it was Deacon (the guy that Jarrett sat with and watched a hawk fly almost 12-feet away from them)—they both sat and talked and chilled for a little while. Deacon spent the night in town, but Jarrett continued onto Sassafras Gap Shelter. When he arrived there, he was the only one in the shelter, and after he was done filtering his water and eating his dinner, he started to realize that that was the first night he had felt a little nervous and he began questioning his fears. He realized that he was scared of being alone, and trying to deal with this, he started to think about all of the people who mean a lot to him, family and friends. At this point, he tried falling asleep, but he just couldn't, he was wide-awake with thoughts on his mind, so he decided to get up from his sleeping bag, and just as he stood up, another hiker walks into the shelter and introduces himself as Creeper. He's called Creeper because he walks slowly on the trail. They both hung out with each other through the night and Jarrett felt a lot better.

April 30th—When he woke up this morning, he hauled ass—put in 20.7-miles to get to Fontana Dam, North Carolina. That's where he is right now. He met up with Brian again (the guy that he met on the Approach Trail with Woodsy and Greg), and he also met up with Iron Horse (the guy who carried Jarrett's backpack and helped him to Gooch Gap Shelter because of his knee) and Hattie Mae (Iron Horse's girlfriend). The four of them took a shuttle van up to the Fontana Dam Hotel—$10/hiker—a thru-hiker special (shuttle-ride and one night stay). The hotel is hooked up with a pool, an all-you-can-eat restaurant, the whole thing. For dinner Jarrett had two salads, a cheeseburger, fries, four pieces of cake and lots of water.

May 1st—Today he stayed at the hotel and just rested up his body. This day is called a zero-day (a day where no mileage is completed). He went swimming with Brian this afternoon and then walked over to the post office to pick up his mail drop. On his way to the post office, he met up with Woodsy again. Woodsy was limping due to a shin-splint. Jarrett told me that he was in a lot of pain, and he's now contemplating getting off the trail because he really misses his girlfriend.

May 2nd—Tomorrow Jarrett is planning on walking into the Great Smoky Mountain National Park. The trail passes through 70-miles of this park.

Jarrett's quote of the week:

"THE HUMAN SOUL NEEDS ACTUAL BEAUTY MORE THAN BREAD."
—Jackie

DAY 18
Journal Entry—
May 2, sunset, Smoky Mountains
<u>I Haven't</u>
I haven't breathed, until I inhaled the fresh mountain air,
  drank, until I dipped my cup into a natural spring,
  eaten, until I tasted mother earth's edibles,
  bathed, until I cleansed myself with the river's water,
  fallen asleep, until the moon kissed me goodnight,
  woken up, until the birds announced the sun's rise,
  lived, until I lived with nature.

<u>Morning Sounds</u>
No Squeaks, Beep, Honk, Boom, Clank,
Rattle, Bang, Pow, Click, Slam, Bam,
Chime, Bleep, Crash.
No Beeps…just tweets.

DAY 21
Journal Entry—
May 5, sunset
Today I saw one bobcat, one bear who trapped us inside a shelter while eating lunch (note: don't eat tuna or sardines while hiking in the Smokies), four horses with horseback riders, and two deer. It rained today, but what a great day for some wildlife.

DAY 22
Journal Entry—
May 6 (Monday), 3 weeks!
Stayin' here at Mountain Mama's (a grocery store, restaurant and bunkhouse at the north end of the Smoky Mountains). Great, great, great cheeseburgers here, lodging is a dump though. Worse than the shelters! Oh well. I'm fed, clean, and my clothes are in the wash. Can't complain.

Just left the Smokies. First 3-days were rough. After a 0-day in Fontana Dam and 6-days of food in my pack…it was really hard to get going on that first day out—especially the initial climb up into the Smokies. The second and third day it rained a lot—rain—wind—rain—wind—fog. Climbed Clingmans Dome that third day—highest peak on the AT (6,643-feet)—couldn't see more than 6-feet in front of you. Also climbed Rocky Top, Tennessee. Need to hear that song again to reconnect. Forth day, nothing but blue-sky sunshine, and I was ready to hike the nicest part of the Smokies. Hiking on the ridgeline (mountain crest-line) all day long. I was on top of the world up there. Nothing but beauty all around me. 20-some odd miles of nothing but pure, beautiful nature—nature in front of me, nature behind me, nature to my right, nature to my left, nature up above and nature down below…it was just amazing…I was surrounded by it all. Surrounded by nature! What a beautiful day of hiking. Today—I just hiked 15-miles to Mountain Mama's, and tomorrow I'm off to Hot Springs, North Carolina—which'll take me about 2-3 days to get to. Just heard the buzzer. My wash is ready. Peace.

From:	Jackie
To:	Friends & Family
Subject:	I spoke to Jarrett
Date:	Tuesday, May 7, 2002, 9:06am

Good morning,

Jarrett just called me this morning. He only had 2 minutes to talk because was on a pay phone that didn't take his calling card and wouldn't accept incoming calls either. However, he did have the chance to say that yesterday he finished walking through the Smoky Mountains and today he's walking towards Hot Spring, North Carolina. He expects to be there in 2-3 days. He said that when he gets to Hot Springs he'll call again. I'll speak to you all then. Have a gr-8 day :)

—Jackie

DAY 23
Journal Entry—
May 7

<u>For Every</u>

For every spring I pass,
    I wish to bathe with you.
For every mountain I climb,
    I wish to relax with you.
For every view I see,
    I wish to share it with you.
For every sunset I glance upon,
    I wish to gaze with you.
For every bird that sings,
    I wish to listen with you.
For every flower I notice,
    I wish to smell it with you.
For every moon and starlit sky I sleep under,
    I wish to dream with you.
For every rock I look at,
    I wish to crack it open and keep half with you.
For every step I take,
    I wish to take it with you.
For every thought I ponder,
    I wish to share it with you.
For every stumble I encounter,
    I wish to laugh it off with you.
For every night I lay down,
    I wish to lay with you.
For every moment I miss you,
    I wish to look beside me and feel I'm with you.
For every butterfly that flies by,
    I wish to chase it with you.

DAY 24
Journal Entry—
May 8, finally sharpened my pencil!!!

Pulled out another quote from Kim's pouch:
    "Dreams are necessary to life."—Anaïs Nin
Yes…but to fulfill one's life, it is necessary to live one's dreams.

From:	Jackie
To:	Friends & Family
Subject:	Message from Jarrett
Date:	Friday, May 10, 2002, 10:14pm

Hi, I just received this message from Jarrett in which he wanted me to pass along to all of you. Enjoy!!!!!

Hello all. I'm at the Hot Springs Public Library. It's next to the elementary school and the kids must be out for recess 'cause there's about 40 little kids running aimlessly around the schoolyard, on top of each other, climbing the swings and slides, yelling, screaming, more running…you know, the typical elementary school recess activities!

Recess…why do some good things in life have to come to an end? Imagine everyday at around 12:25pm, your supervisor, or boss, comes around to your lunch table and dismisses your table, and only your table—because we all got dismissed one table at a time—and you and you co-workers, who all sit at your table, run aimlessly around outside for a half an hour of screaming, kicking, running, swinging, sliding, playing red-rover and kickball with that red rubber bouncy ball that always made that 'BOING' sound whenever you kicked it really hard with your toe. Anyway, wouldn't that be something!

Well, back the library scene:

This town is amazing. It's called Hot Springs because, well, there are hot springs here. You might say to yourself that this seems obvious, but I've been to several towns around this country called Warm Springs, Cold Springs, and other *temperatured*-Springs, and the only spring they ever seem to have is the one when winter is over. That sounded a lot funnier in my head! Moving on…

So I was planning on staying at this hostel called Elmer's, named after a '76 thru-hiker, Elmer (the owner). It's a beautiful house with a great yard, organic garden, hammock, porch, grill, vegetarian meals prepared fresh from his garden…the works! But there's a wedding in town and the whole place is booked up for the weekend. Kind of a bummer, but I've found some other accommodations. Wonderfully enough, this weekend is the Hot Springs River Music Festival and there'll be bluegrass, rock, folk, country and all sorts of other music being played here. The festival is being held at the town's campground, so an entire community of music appreciators will be moving on in for the weekend. I was planning on staying here for just a day, but now I'm embracing this festival to the fullest. Good music, kind folks, camping, drumming, fires…the only thing missing here is all you guys!!!

I've just spent the past week hiking through the Smokies. Beautiful mountains. The first three days it rained quite a bit. No views, especially on top of Clingmans Dome, the highest peak on the AT, and Rocky Top, Tennessee. Some of you may know the song—Rocky Top. I only knew the chorus, and I sang it over and over and over again as I climbed my way up and over that rocky top.

Third day in the Smokies—Iron Horse, Hattie Mae and I took a break and had some lunch inside one of the shelters. All of the shelters on the AT are built out of wood, and they only have three sides, exposing an entire forth side to all of the natural elements, however in the Smokies, all of the shelters have been built out of stone, and they all have a chain-link fence running across the forth side because of the high bear population in the park. Well brilliantly, while we were all inside one of these shelters taking a break for lunch, I opened up a package of tuna fish and Hattie Mae opens up a can of sardines, and about five minutes later, Iron Horse jumps up and scrambles over to the fence to lock us in, and the bear, with his/her nose up in the air, out. This bear must have weighed 350-400 pounds, easily. So what do you think we do first? Iron Horse and I immediately take out our cameras and start snapping away as if we were at the zoo. The only difference here was that we were the ones on display.

I guess if the roles were reversed between humans and animals, and all of the animals spent their weekends at the human zoo to see what us humans do whenever we're approached by an animal, all of the penguins and bears and caterpillars would stop to watch us take pictures of them.

Tangent thought—happens all the time.

Back to the shelter—so there we were, all locked up in the shelter for about an hour or so. The bear, despite its size, didn't seem all that threatening. It only wanted our food. Bears are pretty scared of humans out here. Matter of fact, everything out here is scared of humans. As I walk the trail, I hear animals and insects fleeing for their lives in fear of some mass destruction I may cause on their environment. I wonder where all that stems from???

So finally we started clapping our hands and banging on the fence, but the bear wouldn't leave—it just continued pacing back and forth in front of the shelter. Iron Horse tried 'shewing' it off by waving his hands up in the air, but that didn't work either—it only gave Hattie Mae and I a good laugh. Then I remembered Carey Lewis, the 15-year old Boy Scout that I met back in Gooch Gap Shelter. He taught me how to scare off bears. He said that they don't like the sound of metal being banged up against each other, so I started rattling my rings up against the chain-link fence, and then just like that, the bear ran back off into the woods.

The whole experience was pretty remarkable. It was really amazing to just sit back in the protection of a shelter, know that we were all safe, and just watch, observe and connect to a bear out in the wild. It truly was an amazing experience.

Forth day in the Smokies—sun was shining, birds were singing, nothing but blue-sky sunshine. I haven't seen the blue sky in 3-whole days, so you can just imagine how I reacted to it that morning. This stretch was the most beautiful section of the Smokies, and the AT, so far for me. 20-miles of nothing but ridgeline hiking. No climbing up or down, no valleys, no peaks, just walking along the crest of the mountains, for 20-miles, with views of the Smoky Mountains, hawks, deer, birds, trees, rivers, flowers…life on either side of me. To my right…beauty, to my left…more beauty, and nothing but endless beauty in front and behind me. What a great day of hiking. Such a great day that I decided to continue on by myself (leaving Iron Horse and Hattie Mae behind in the distance). I just spent the past 3 days/nights solo-hiking and simply blissing out with myself out here.

I found myself doing some really incredible things on my own. At one shelter I constructed an entire drum set using different sized rocks and logs to create various sounds. I found two sturdy branches and banged them on my drum set for about an hour or so. My beats traveled through the mountains, echoed right back at me, and then traveled through the mountains once again. It really was amazing!

I then found myself standing in a Tai Chi stance, trying to catch the hundreds of flying gnats with my one bare hand. I caught three in about an hour. Trying to teach myself how to focus out here. Wasn't too successful. Need to watch The Karate Kid again for more lessons with Mr. Miyagi.

The next day I started singing, no wait, I started yelling every song that I knew. For about two hours I sung every Cat Stevens song I knew, and I really let 'em out. Walking through the mountains, singing *Wild World, Peace Train, If You Want To Sing Out, Sing Out*…every song I knew. Well eventually, I came upon this one shelter and saw a lady sitting there by a tree and reading her book. I didn't want to be disrespectful, so I lowered my voice, and as soon as I did, she tells me that she's been listening to me sing for the past hour through these mountains and that she's been so comically entertained by it all. Her name is Lucky Laura, a thru-hiker from '95, back here to section-hike the Smokies (her favorite part of the AT) for her vacation. She told me that she comes back here to reconnect with what she once found out on the trail during her thru-hike, and then after saying that, she looked up into the trees, took in a deep breath of fresh mountain air, started to tear, and then offered me some hot chocolate.

That night I spent the evening inside of a shelter on top of Walnut Mountain. The sun was just starting to set and the wind was so powerful up there. I opened up my arms, leaned into the wind, and started twirling around and dancing to the songs of the wind. I moved with all the power of the air up there—wherever it went, so did I. It was like I was one with the wind, one with the air, one with the movement.

Of all the hikers I've met out here, I especially connected to one in particular. His name is Katu, The Whistling Jackrabbit. That's his trail-name because he's a swift hiker and he whistles throughout the day. He's a Japanese journalist who is hiking the AT and writing a book about his experiences. We stayed at one of the shelters together and chatted about all kinds of issues. We started to really connect when we spoke about how we don't believe in the levels of hierarchy regarding people, animals, plants, soil…we believe that we are all one coming from the same one source. We took such a strong interest in each other that he interviewed me for his book and took some pictures of me as well. He also gave me his address and phone number and invited me to stay with his family if I ever make it out to Japan. I would've loved to have walked the entire trail with Katu, but he's on his own trip with his literature. Beside Katu, I'm constantly meeting amazingly inspiring folks out here, however Katu and I sparked a connection that you rarely embrace when meeting someone for the first time. He's a real special man.

I'm having the time of my life out here. Physically wandering, which leads to mental wandering…with no restrictions, influences, or pressures. My mind is free to travel anywhere…very liberating and inspiring. As my mind travels freely with thoughts, my emotions are touched in all different ways, depending on what flows through my mind as I wander on this trail. And this leads to enlightened spiritual freedoms. Amazing, isn't it?

I've been given the trail-name Patience, however I spell it PACEnce. I think it fits me just fine. It's nice to have a name live up to your actions rather than your actions living up to your name!

Well, I'm going back into town to get some food—the festival is starting up soon.

I'll be heading north through the Cherokee and Pisqua Mountains to Erwin, Tennessee, and from there, I think I'll find a ride up north to Damascus, Virginia for the annual Appalachian Trail thru-hiker event called Trail Days. More music, parades, food, backpacking seminars, outdoor gear outfitters, the works…all catered to and for the thru-hikers.

The journey continues…within all of us, for we are all on a trail of some sort!

Harmony—Pacence

DAY 31
Journal Entry—
May 15

Struggles, challenges, forks, roads, decisions, satisfying myself, satisfying others, time, age, thoughts, feelings, right, wrong, parents, friends, truth, life, success, meaning, passion, searching, harmony, lust, desire, finding, flowers, grass, sky, live, young, old, one, mental, spiritual, water, fire, decisions, noises, voices, sounds, sight, color, smell, feel, growth, cleanse, sage, smoke, lullabies, what is it, what it is, do I, don't I, should I, shouldn't I, does it matter, doesn't it matter, sex, friends, relationships, people, music, noise, decisions, roads, forks, challenges, struggles, nowhere...

—somewhere.

From:	Jackie
To:	Friends & Family
Subject:	Message from Jarrett
Date:	Thursday, May 16, 2002, 1:11pm

Hi everyone—here's another message from Jarrett.

One week later…still in Hot Springs. It's Thursday, May 16th. I initially arrived here last Thursday with the intention of taking a 0-day on Friday and then heading back to the trail on Saturday. This all changed when I found out about the Hot Springs River Music Festival and after a long phone call with Bari. With a music festival in town, natural hot spring mineral water baths, a farmer's market, the city of Ashville only 45-minutes away, blue-sky sunshine, the Smoky Mountains, and a local bridge to jump off from and into a river with a swimming hole that's 70-feet deep, it was pretty hard for Bari not to jump on the next plane and fly down here for the weekend—and that's exactly what happened. She found a special offer with Continental Airlines, some weekend getaway offer, and flew into Ashville Saturday morning. I asked around town for a ride to the airport and this one lady named Sonja, who was eating at the Bridge Street Café & Inn, was pretty sure that her husband was driving into the city that day. I told her which motel I was lodging at and within an hour a note gets passed under my door saying that I should call her to make some arrangements. The next day, Jerry, her husband, picks me up early in the morning and we head out to Ashville together. What a generous man. Turns out he's the chairman of the board for community service projects and events in Hot Springs. He's a real respected man in town. The kind of person everyone knows, and he, in return, is friendly with everybody…genuinely of course! After talking with him for awhile about our lives and experiences, he assures me that if I'm ever interested in moving to North Carolina and pursuing some work in environmental education, he would be a great resource in helping me out with my search.

I'm running out of time here with my free on-line thru-hiker privileges, so I'll be swift in the turn of events.

Bari flies in, we spend the day in Ashville together, wonderful city, drove back to Hot Springs, music festival through the night, great grilled cheeses, quesadillas, people, and the music was pretty good as well, we walked around town, talked with lots of people, stayed in a cabin and spent some time in the hot springs during a storm that was blowing in. Her flight was cancelled Monday evening (due to the storm), so we ended up staying at Elmer's Hostel and she flew out Tuesday morning. That day I made it to the edge of town (where the trail picks back up), called my parents and Jackie from a local pay phone to say hello, took two steps towards the trail and figured that I was never going to make it to Damascus, Virginia on time for Trail Days if I had walked there. So I turned back around, headed back to Elmer's, offered to work there for a couple days in exchange for room and board, no problem. Been working here for the past couple of days on his farm, farming and helping him build his all energy-efficient, completely self-sustaining home. After a day or two of work, Elmer offers me a job, an open-ended job, whenever I'd like to start and whenever I'd like to work until. Living arrangements at the hostel and mellow work around the farm.

Decisions, confusion, choices, trails, paths, forks, life, should I, shouldn't I, mmm, what to do? What to do?

Found a ride up to Damascus. Leaving this afternoon, heading north to a bluegrass gathering at a local barn and then spending the night at another hostel up there. No charge, food included. Friday, heading to Trail Days, which is an event that caters to and for thru-hikers, or any hiker, the entire hiking community, I guess. Music, parades, talent shows, gear exchanges, seminars, workshops, and food, tons and tons of food. And hikers, new, old, hundreds of them, possibly thousands, from what people are talking about. Earl Shaffer, the first AT thru-hiker (back in 1948), passed away a week or two ago. Probably will have some memorial service in his honor, which is expected to bring even more folks to the event. Everyone tents out by the river, hundreds of tents, a scene out of Woodstock, I hear.

Need some time away from Hot Springs to see where I continue on from here.

Trail taking on new meanings. It's only as physical as I make it. No matter what I decide or where I end up, I'm still on the trail.

Having faith in life, it all unfolds before you. Listening to what is best for me, not getting caught up with the herd mentality.

I miss and love you all.

Harmony—Pacence

DAY 33

Journal Entry—
May 17, sun is still high

Let me take you back to an experience about loneliness.

Tough day of hiking. Stormy, rainy, windy, cold, wet, but in all that, I found my peace on the other side of that mountain. Rain stopped, wind died down, sky opened up and sun shined everywhere…peacefulness! Made my way to the shelter. Big day. 20+miles. Usually I turn the corner to the opening of a shelter and folks are already in there doing their thing. Not this time. This time I turned that corner to an empty shelter. It was a bit run down and dark inside, but I didn't pay too much attention to those details…yet.

It's amazing. You hike all day. Up, down, straight, right, left, rain, sun, clouds, winds, birds, hiking, hiking, hiking. You'd think you'd get to that shelter and just reeelax. But I don't. I unpack, filter water, cook dinner, clean myself, hang my food, da da da da da…and when all my chores are finally done, that's when it sets in. No more activities to distract myself from what I initially felt when I first stumbled upon this shelter. I'll get to this feeling in a moment. So there I sat, clean, hydrated, full, sleeping bag all rolled out and 2½-hours left of sunlight…I'm scared, fear sets in, I'm in a shelter very far out in the middle of the mountains, far from any town, road, home, far from any hint or glimmer of society—society—a place in which I'd feel safer? That's interesting in itself. Society is what drove me out here (or least one of the things that did) and now that I'm here, I feel too far away from there. And *there* is where I'd feel safer? What's going on here? What am I scared of? Where does my fear lie? Is it the mice? Am I scared of the mice running all over and through my sleeping bag…no, they're just mice. Is it a bear that I'm scared of? Do I fear a bear smelling out my leftovers, my food, my garbage, my breath, me? Do I fear a bear smelling its way into this shelter and mistaking me for a huge purple (color of my sleeping bag) Snickers bar? Not really. The chainsaw massacre! That's it. I'm afraid of some kooky mountain man chopping me up at night and storing me in his basement icebox for some sick pleasure. What! I can't believe I just thought that! I can't believe that just ran through my mind! My mind! Whose mind is it? Is it mine? I don't want to be thinking these horrible thoughts, but I am. Why? Why, who, what, when, where were these ideas fed into my mind? Back in society…movies, newspapers, TV programs, horror stories…society—the place where I'm mistaking fearlessness. The place where I'd feel safer. The place where I'd be free of these thoughts. Everything is backwards. What's going on here? What am I scared of? It's not the mice. I'm not scared of bears…yet. And this whole masked murderer thing is only a thought stemming from my conditioned mind. So what is it then? What is it that I'm afraid of? I had a great hike today, I feel good, I'm well fed, I'm in a shelter, and I'm sitting here on this platform feakin' out. Why can't I just relax, enjoy, breathe, focus? I'm the only one in here and I'm creating all of these ridiculous scenarios…that's it! That's what I'm scared of. That's what I fear. It's not the scenarios. It's not the created thoughts. It's the fact and the everlasting idea that I'm the only one in here…I'm alone. Loneliness. I fear loneliness. That's what I'm scared of. I'm scared of being alone. Oh no…I should be grateful that I just tapped into this problem, but instead, I feel even more wilder in my fears. Avoid it. Run away from it. Pretend it doesn't exist. Go into your sleeping bag and forget it. Zip down…get in…zip up, eyes closed, now sleep. Nooowww sleep. Sleep already. You can either fall asleep and forget about your problems or stay up and deal with it. Now what's it gonna be? "Mom, dad, Jackie, Bari, Peter and Phoebe, Alison, Josh and Jen, Mike and Ginny, Kim, Zach, friends, family." Ahhh. Happy thoughts. Where did all these people come from? Who cares, they're here with me now, all of them, here in my thoughts. Here with me, to support, comfort, nurture and be with me. I feel better now. I'm calming down. I'm breathing, relaxing. I'm not going to forget about my problems. I'm not going to fall asleep with it still being so bright out. I'm going to deal with my problems, internalize it, figure them out and deal with it. No matter how hard this road's gonna be. Roads…trails—roads/trails/trail/road/road/trail. Roads in my mind/trail for my body/paths for my heart/vessels for my soul. That's what this is all about…this trail…this experience. Wandering by foot. Wandering by mind. Dealing with myself, my issues, my worries, my insecurities, me, myself. Right now I feel lonely, and I hurt because of it. Loneliness is not okay with me and I'm going to start dealing with it. Zip down, get out, stand up…let's read the shelter register and see/feel the vibe from what others have felt in the past. Reaching for it…"Hello…uh…I'm Creeper." Hello, I'm Jarrett—I turn around and answer—people been calling me Pacence. "Nice to meet you." You too.

I thought that night was going to be the first one spent alone in a shelter…it wasn't, just the first night to tap into loneliness. I've spent the past three nights alone in shelters…loved all three. I've conquered my fear. In a time that I thought I needed someone most, I found myself. No sooner did I find myself, a thru-hiker walks in.

Thank you—

From:	Jackie
To:	Friends & Family
Subject:	Message from Jarrett
Date:	Sunday, May 19, 2002, 8:29am

Hi everyone,

Today I finally was home when Jarrett called. He is in Damascus, Virginia for Trail Days. He didn't think he'd make it there from Hot Springs in time (if he walked), so he hitched a ride instead. He's going to get a ride back down to Hot Springs after the event and continue walking on the trail from there. Enjoy this email from Jarrett below.....

I'm in Damascus, Virginia for the thru-hiker festival called Trail Days…music, food, parades, camping, drum-circles, fires, free gear and repair, raffles, and of course, hikers…hundreds…maybe thousands of hikers, and we all congregated for the first time at the Thru-Hiker Parade up Main Street…it truly was a magical experience. We were all one out there, hiking together through town. I can't find the words to explain the energy of that parade, but I can definitely say that tears and smiles were expressed by just about everyone who joined. Trail-life sure is something to experience.

I hitched a ride up here from Hot Springs. Got a ride from a trucker in a big-rig. Always wanted to sit/ride in one of those monster 16-wheelers, and finally got the chance. Rode with a great man who just got laid off work in a days notice. Now he's a trucker and loves being on the road. He took me west to Route 81. From there, I got picked up by a Brazilian family who was heading back home to Boston after vacationing down in Texas. Minimal English, but just enough to communicate. They listened to Bob Marley the whole way up while their 5-year old daughter sang Brazilian pre-school songs to me. Got dropped off about 70-miles north and then another lady drove me 10-miles east to Damascus. I asked her for a ride while she was filling up her car at a gas station. After I asked her for a ride, she holds out her hand and says, "I'll make you a deal. If you don't kill me, I won't kill you." So we shook on it and off we went. Been camping out here since Thursday night with a family of thru-hikers (related by experience) that I've met along the way.

It's truly magical here. Everyone refers to everyone else by their trail-names, even the store workers, vendor volunteers, restaurant staff and post office clerks all ask for our trail-names in conversation and matters dealing with business. Some names are as common as Randy, to as far out as Rebel With A Cause, and every-thing in between. It's really amazing to realize just how many hikers I've met along the way, and how many of them have already made a positive impact on my hike—this realization all came to a head for me here at the festival. They're all here. Every one of those hikers that I've either walked with, cooked with, drank with, slept with, watched sunsets, sunrises and views with, lived with...are all here to reconnect with a hug and a smile. There was a Thru-Hiker Talent Show earlier this morning and this one lady sang a song about what makes the trail. She sang about how it's not the mountains or the valleys or the peaks that make the trail. It's not the birds or bears or bobcats that make the trail. Not the views or sunrises or sunsets. Not the hiking or sleeping outside or bathing in the streams that make up the trail. It's not the towns or parks or communities. And it's not even the continuous footpath that stretches all the way from Georgia to Maine that makes up the Appalachian Trail. It's the people...the hikers, the souls, the hearts, minds, bodies, the spirit of travelers that make up this trail...and man, when she sung that, did she hit it on the nail! I couldn't have stopped myself from tearing if I tried—no one could. That lady struck a cord that resonated deep within us all, and when I looked all around me at everyone sitting there listening to her, I felt exactly what she was singing about—I felt the entire community of Appalachian Trail thru-hikers—and as I felt this entire thru-hiking community, I no longer viewed us all as individual thru-hikers, I saw us all as one continuous thru-hiker thru-hiking one continuous trail. It was simply beautiful. Just beautiful!

Earl Shaffer, the AT's first thru-hiker, passed away this week and there's a memorial service for him in a few minutes. So I'm signing off for now and riding back to Hot Springs tomorrow. From there, I'll be continuing north. The journey continues!

Feelin' groovy—Pacence

DAY 37
Journal Entry—
May 21
<u>Why Can't I</u>
Why can't I sail on land,
          walk on water,
          sleep while awake,
          live while I die?

Why can't I run while still,
          sit while stand,
          inspire while desire,
          will you take me,
          am I hired?

I am what I am,
      so don't mind me,
          it just had to be,
            when my heart didn't see.

And now I've learned, regained myself.

From:	Jackie
To:	Friends & Family
Subject:	Jarrett
Date:	Thursday, May 30, 2002, 5:16pm

Hi everyone,

I know it's been a little while, but I just heard from Jarrett and this is what he has told me.

Trail Days got him really excited to get back on the trail. He hitched a ride down to Hot Springs and when he got back on the trail, he walked crazy miles per day (25-30 miles/day). The weather has been great. He met up with a family of four, two little kids ages 6 and 8, who's thru-hiking the trail. Their family's trail-name is The Idaho Four (because they're from Idaho and have four members in their family). The kids are being home-schooled on the trail, so they're all carrying textbooks with them. Jarrett said that one night the 6-year old boy built a fire for everyone at a shelter. Jarrett walked with this family for a bit and then he met up with another thru-hiker named Pete (Nappy is his trail-name because he takes lots of naps), who he's been hiking with for the past 100-miles. Jarrett said that he finally feels like he's made his first real trail-friend. Nappy is from Rhode Island—Jarrett described him as a total floater. Perfect for Jarrett.

The first couple days Jarrett and Nappy walked through varying thunderstorms. They made their way on top of a bald (a low elevation mountain surrounded by forest, yet bare of trees at the top, typically covered with meadows) that's been grazed over by cows, and when they finally got up there, they noticed that the cows weren't cows at all, but rather they were long-horned bulls—and they were standing all over the trail. Jarrett and Nappy were so scared. He said that the horns on these bulls were huge. Nonetheless, Nappy was wearing his *red* Marmot rain jacket, so he took it off and they continued hiking with caution. They wanted to take a picture of the bulls but they figured that the flash would aggravate them into a charge, so they just kept on walking slowly by them and nothing bad happened, although they did find themselves surrounded by piles and plies of bullshit. Jarrett said it was the biggest bunch of shit he's ever seen, and now he fully understands the real meaning behind something that's truly bullshit.

On the evening of the 25th, Jarrett and Nappy walked together through the night. It was their first time night-hiking and they both loved it. The sky was clear and it was the night just before the full moon, so it was a great time to walk. They both had their headlamps on and Jarrett said that it was a bit scary at first. He kept his head down most of the time, shining his light only on the trail, but sometimes he would shine it off into the woods and see all sorts of eyes reflecting back at him. He heard someone say that for every animal you see in the woods, a hundred animals are staring right back at you. Even though he continued walking with this thought in mind, he slowly started to become more and more comfortable with how peaceful it was to walk with the night. He said that all you see is what your light illuminates. All you hear is the sound of the crickets. And all you smell is the earth cooling down. Everything else is quite and asleep. He really felt at peace with all of this, but he'd occasionally get startled when he'd hear a squirrel darting off into the woods. He said that every sound is so exaggerated at night, so a tiny squirrel sounded like a huge bear.

The next couple of days they saw snakes, frogs, a beautiful deer, and they came across an amazing animal that looked like a cross between a rabbit and a squirrel—looked like a jackalope he said.

One day Jarrett and Nappy split up to re-supply their food. Jarrett went to the post office to pick up his mail drop that I had mailed to him, and Nappy walked about 2-miles out of town to a small grocery store. When Nappy finally got there, the store was closed down, and that really put him in a bad mood because he had just walked 2-miles out of his way and now he had to walk another 2-miles back up to the trail. He started to feel like it was going to be a real bad day for him, so he began saying to himself, "Alright, calm down, it's no big deal. Just be patient. That's all I need. I just need patience." And by the time he made it back up to the trail, guess who was getting dropped off from hitchhiking out of town at that exact moment? Pacence! It made Nappy's day. All Nappy said he needed was patience, and he got just what he asked for! When Nappy told Jarrett this story, that's when Jarrett knew that he had made his first trail-friend.

Last night, Jarrett and Nappy hiked through the night once again. They crossed the Tennessee-Virginia border at 5am this morning and made it to Damascus, Virginia at 7am. Jarrett said that it was so peaceful walking into that town at that hour. The mist was rising from the grass, the sun was just coming up, the birds were all welcoming their arrival, and the people were just starting to begin their day.

Before Jarrett left for the trail, he worked as a naturalist with an outdoor educational program called BOCES on Long Island, New York. He used to facilitate team-building activities that would teach kids how to build self-confidence, group-support and teamwork. He taught these lessons using a high-ropes course in the trees and a 32-foot climbing wall, and he'd always tell the kids that the object of these two activities is not to get to the end of the course or to the top of the wall, but rather to set realistic goals for themselves and try to reach their own level of success. He'd always recommend setting three goals and then aiming to reach each one at a time. Jarrett used this same strategy for himself when beginning the Appalachian Trail. Before he started hiking, he set three goals for himself as well. His first goal was to reach Damascus, Virginia—so he just conquered that! Now he's aiming for his second goal—Bear Mountain, New York. And then finally, his third and final goal will be to climb up Mount Katahdin in Maine!

Today, Jarrett and Nappy are taking a zero-day and resting up. Jarrett said that whenever you get into a town all you want to do is take a shower and do laundry, but this gets kind of tricky because sometimes the shower and the laundromat are in two different places. So here's the dilemma. Do you take a shower first and then put your dirty clothes on your clean body to go to the laundromat? Or do you go to the laundromat first and then put your clean clothes on your dirty body to go take a shower? Well, this is what he does. First he takes a shower. Then he wraps a towel around his waist and walks his dirty clothes up to the laundromat. This may sound easy, but this time in Damascus, he was staying at a hostel in a local church and the only towel they had left was a small skimpy pink and purple striped one. So that's exactly what he had to wear, and when he walked his laundry up Main Street to the laundromat, all these people started whistling at him, honking at him and cheering him on. He was a bit embarrassed, but I guess that's all a part of life on the trail.

Jarrett hasn't brushed his hair since he started hiking. He said that for one to fully experience nature, one has to completely let go of the civilized self. So he started to let go of his civilized self by letting go of his physical appearance, and after a month and a half of letting his appearance go, his hair is now starting to dread—there's one dread lock forming in the back. After he told me this, he then shouted into the phone, "RASTA MON VIBRATION!" and said that he's now starting to feel the Marley within.

He ended the phone call by saying:

"Life is perfect, it really is.
It is so absolutely perfect when you become aware of what is going on."
—Jackie

DAY 47
Journal Entry—
5-31

Left Damascus this morning. Nappy wanted to stay in town a bit longer, but I wanted to continue on. We both knew that we'd see each other again up the trail. You constantly meet back up with thru-hikers out here—I guess that's the nature of life when people are traveling in the same one direction. You're bound to meet up with them again sometime along the way.

DAY 54
Journal Entry—
6-7

Today was the first day I lost the trail. I had to take this really bad shit and I was only 1-mile away from the shelter. I held it in for as long as I could and I thought that I could make it to the next privy, but I just couldn't hold it in anymore, so I took a hard right off the trail and began running downhill for about 100-yards or so. I dropped my pack down next to a tree, dropped my shorts, and then my bowels. After I was done, I started walking back up to the trail, and after walking for what seemed like too far, I soon realized that I was lost. I couldn't find the trail anywhere. I looked down below me and thought I'd be able to see a path, but I couldn't. I looked up above and thought the same thing, but it was impossible to see any trail with all that low ground brush. So I headed back down to the tree where I dropped my pack, and when I looked all around me, I noticed that I was standing at the bottom of a circular valley where all of the mountains sloped uphill in every direction all around me. I thought that I had walked back up to where I first ran down, but back up could've been anywhere! So I started figuring to myself, "If I'm walking north on a trail, and I take a hard right, then I've headed east, so in order to get back up to the trail, I have to head west." I looked down at the compass that was dangling around my neck, orientated myself, and then started walking in that direction, but still, I couldn't find the trail anywhere. I was lost. I knew I was lost. I could just feel it. I started pacing around in small circle. Thoughts started running through my mind, "Okay, I have three days worth of food in my pack, a full bottle of water, a tent, a sleeping bag, matches…I'll be fine, for a couple days at least." And then suddenly the worries began to follow, "I can't believe it! How am I lost? How did this happen? I just ran off the trail for a couple moments. How did I get lost?"—and at that very moment, I looked right down at my feet and saw the most precious thing I had ever seen in my entire life—a little baby deer all curled up in a little tiny ball, resting there in the middle of the tall green grass. It was the most humbling sight I could've ever asked for. There I was, with several days of provisions in my pack, feeling lost in the woods, concerned and a bit nervous—and there was that little baby deer, all curled up in a little ball, still, silent, and without its mother. It looked so fragile, so delicate, so passive lying there, and as I watched it for a brief moment, that's when I began to realize that even though we had both appeared to be lost in the woods, I was the one feeling like I didn't belong in nature—and at that exact moment of realization, I gently stepped away from the baby deer, took out my whistle, and started blowing it and yelling out for help, "Help! I'm lost. Can anybody hear me?"—and I continued blowing my whistle several times more, and then I began to yell once again, "Help! Help! I'm lost!"—and about 10-feet away from me, I hear a voice, "Hey, over here!" I turned around and looked. A hiker was coming right up the trail just beside me. I couldn't believe it. My body was standing only several feet away from the trail, but my mind had wondered miles and miles off into the woods.

When I stepped back onto the trail, I looked back down into the valley where that baby deer still laid, and I felt green with envy. I began to think to myself, "I want to be like that deer...I want to feel like I belong in nature, even if that means I'm lost in the woods!"

DAY 56
Journal Entry—
6-9

Crossed the Eastern Continental Divide at Sinking Creek Mountain (3,450-feet). Stayin' here at Pickle Branch Shelter. Met up with Iron Horse and Hattie Mae again. It's so great to see them here. Iron Horse was hanging his food bag up in the trees. He wrapped a cord around this large rock and hurled it over a tall sturdy branch so that he could collect it on the other side, but when that rock came whipping around the branch, it almost swung right into him, knocking him out. Hattie Mae started cracking up, which was a nice relief to see, since I'm sensing a bit of tension coming from her. Not sure what it is, but she seems to be a bit frustrated with Iron Horse right now.

DAY 61
Journal Entry—
6-14

Been slackpacking (hiking without a backpack, which is transported up the trail by a trail-angel in town) with Iron Horse and Hattie Mae for the past several days. It's been so much fun. What a rush! Running through the woods without your pack on. So light and free. So exhilarating! You feel like a wild animal out here with all those trees whipping right by you. Hattie Mae has been taking it easy since her blisters have been bothering her, but she's still walking fast behind Iron Horse and I while we've been running on the trail, jumping over rocks and branches, racing up the mountains, sprinting along the ridgeline and darting back down the other side. It's been so much fun. Laughing and hollering while running. It's so easy to laugh when you're running wildly through the woods…but I'd imagine it's just as hard to smile when you're walking behind with blisters on your feet.

DAY 64
Journal Entry—
6-17

I've really enjoyed hiking with Iron Horse and Hattie Mae, but this morning, I just had to leave them behind at the Priest Shelter. Last night they got into a real nasty fight with each other about some lightweight-backpacking stove they had just purchased in town. Hattie Mae was really hungry after a long day of hiking, and Iron Horse just couldn't get the water boiled, so she made some nasty remark to him, and he just lost it on her. That was the first time I heard anyone curse out here on the trail. It was really strange to hear those words out here. Curse words just don't seem to fit in nature.

Anyway, it can't be easy for them. Iron Horse has always wanted to thru-hike the Appalachian Trail, and as for Hattie Mae, well, she just wanted to be with him and not be left alone for 6-months—that's why she's out here—and that can't be easy. I can't imagine thru-hiking this trail for anyone else other than myself. Hiking over 2000-miles just to be with your lover has gotta be tough, and it's gotta be just as tough for Iron Horse as well—hiking all these miles with all that extra weight on his consciousness. Thru-hiking this trail with a partner has got to either make you or break you, and right now, even though they seem to be breaking, I truly believe that what they need is to fully break down before they can completely make up—and that's exactly why I've decided to leave them behind early this morning. Breaking down and making up is something they just have to do on their own.

I just passed a sign by the National Park Service that read:

Appalachian Trail

The Appalachian Trail crisscrosses the Blue Ridge Parkway for 100 miles in Virginia. Farther south, it winds through the Great Smoky Mountains. The trail usually follows the crest of the Appalachian chain, occasionally descending into scenic valleys. The trail's highest point, 6,643 feet, is at Clingmans Dome on the North Carolina-Tennessee border. Its lowest elevation, 124 feet, occurs at Bear Mountain Crossing in New York.

Stretching 2,050 miles from Mt. Katahdin in central Maine to Springer Mountain in northern Georgia, the Appalachian Trail is the longest marked footpath in the world. Begun in 1922, the trail traverses 14 states, including 541 miles in Virginia and more than 200 miles in North Carolina. Hikers who complete the trek visit eight national forests and five national park areas.

DAY 65
Journal Entry—
June 18, right here, right now

Waynesboro, Virginia. Campin' at the YMCA campground. Just got off the phone with Bari. Conversation grew silent. Couldn't say anything more. Couldn't tell her what she wanted to hear about the future. Could only say what I know for sure about the present—and in the present moment, all I know for sure is what I want right now. I have no idea what I'm going to want after the trail—that's three months from now. I only know what I want right here, right now—and right here, right now, I know that I want to be with her—but that's not what she wanted to hear. She wanted to hear what I'm going to want after the trail—and that's why the conversation grew silent. That's why I couldn't say anything more. And that's why she broke up with me.

I knew I was going to lose her, but I just couldn't tell her something I didn't know for sure. It's unfair of me to talk about a future that can easily change with experience. I'm going through so many different changes out here that I can't even imagine what I'm going to be feeling when I'm done with this trail. The only thing I know for sure is what I'm feeling right now—and that's all I can honestly talk about. I'm not thinking about a reality that exists in the future. I'm not thinking about a reality that existed in the past. I'm only focusing on a reality that's existing right here in the present—and that's the only way I'm able to fully embrace the moment.

I understand why she broke up with me. I understand that she wanted to know what I'm going to want after the trail. And I understand that she didn't want to wait around for someone who might not be there for her in the end. But what I don't understand is why would you leave someone today for what might happen tomorrow? I believe that if you truly love someone today, you'll love that person tomorrow—not the other way around. I don't believe in loving someone today based upon their future love for you tomorrow. That seems backwards to me. But I guess sometimes in life, love calls for a certain level of insurance—and because I couldn't insure my future love for her, Bari couldn't invest her present love in me. But I don't blame her. She made the right decision. She knew that I couldn't offer her words about a time that doesn't exist right now. Words are easy. Actions are reality. And right now, the reality of my actions is that I'm embracing my current realty.

DAY 66
Journal Entry—
June 19

Just entered the Shenandoah National Park. Been hiking with Me-Tree and You-Tree (two thru-hikers), originally called The Trees, but after having an identity crisis, one Tree said to the other Tree, "How about *you* be You-Tree, and *me*, I'll be Me-Tree."—and that's just how they became who they are. They're both 6'4, long-limbed, tall, thin, super friendly and most generous. I met them last night at the YMCA campground. They borrowed a barbeque from someone in town and cooked a huge feast for all the thru-hikers that were camping out there. They said that after receiving so much love from the trail, this is their way to start offering some back. I spoke with Me-Tree most of the time while You-Tree was busy cooking, but then later in the night, we all sat down together at a picnic table with some other thru-hikers and I listened to You-Tree and Jaberwoki (another thruhiker who just received her trail-name that night) sing Joni Mitchell songs.

This morning, just before Me-Tree and You-Tree were about to get into a car and hitch a ride back to the trail, I ran over to them and offered a gift of my appreciation for the feast they offered us last night. I tied up a few sticks of incense, a couple sticks of candles, and my bundle of sage with a piece of hemp cord. Me-Tree asked me if I wanted to ride back to the trail with them, so I sprinted back to my tent, broke it down in seconds, jammed everything into my backpack and hopped right into that car with them. We all got dropped off at the trailhead just outside Waynesboro, Virginia, hiked to the Shenandoah National Park entrance, self-registered for our camping permits, and have been singing *Me and Julio Down by the Schoolyard* all morning long. We just finished eating lunch while overlooking the Shenandoah Mountains and sharing our food. I have a strong feeling that these are The Trees I've been looking for!

DAY 69
Journal Entry—
June 22

Just ate at a restaurant on Skyline Drive (a road that runs 105-miles north and south along the crest of the Blue Ridge Mountains in Shenandoah National Park). Me-Tree ordered a garden burger with bacon on it. Sounded crazy, but good, so I ordered one as well. It was so tasty…and so were the blackberry milkshakes. The Shenandoahs are beautiful. The views up here are just amazing. Last night we night-hiked. Hiked along an overlook that had incredible views of the city lights down below. We stopped and looked out, started screaming the song *Keep on Rockin' in the Free World*, and when we continued hiking on, about 10-feet in front of us was a huge group of kids sleeping alongside the trail in the their sleeping bags. They must've been on some school trip or something. Their counselors, or teachers, probably told them all to keep still and to not make a single sound. I can't imagine what they must've thought of us up there. Hope they weren't too scared. Probably weren't. Probably thought we were hilarious!

You-Tree, Me-Tree and I got into a really good conversation today—as usual. We notice that when people meet each other on the trail, the first questions they usually ask each other are, "What's your name, where are you from, and how old are you?" But we feel like these questions don't really tell you *who* a person is, they only tell you the details about *what* they are—and details only describe a person's outer surface—but when we first meet someone, we want to know about their inner essence. So we started to think about what would be the perfect opening question that would bring our awareness to this inner essence of who a person really is, not what they are, but who they are—and so this is what we came up with—"What do you believe?" That's it. Plain and simple. Not, "What do you believe *in*?" but simply, "What do you believe?" We figured that if we asked people what they believed in, then they'd probably immediately start talking about religion, or god—and that would be just fine—but if we simply asked them, "What do you believe?" then the question is opened up to more possibilities. We haven't asked anyone this question yet, just each other…and so far, we all believe the same one thing—LOVE!

From:	Jackie
To:	Friends & Family
Subject:	I finally spoke to Jarrett—how long has it been?????
Date:	Tuesday, June 25, 2002, 8:05am

Hi everyone,

I finally got a call from Jarrett today. This is what he had to say:

Last week (6/18) he met two guys who are called The Trees. Me-Tree is from Maine and You-Tree is from Ohio. They're both tall and skinny, and they both started hiking the trail together. That night they camped out at a YMCA campground and had a huge barbeque with 15 other thru-hikers. They were eating and singing the *YMCA* song all night long—a little delirious don't ya think?????

Jarrett and Me-Tree spent most of the evening together. Me-Tree offered Jarrett a slice of watermelon and they started talking for hours about all sorts of things—starting with a common past experience about how they both once got rid of all their needless material possessions. Jarrett told Me-Tree that when he once lived in San Luis Obispo, he had a Yard Trade (not a Yard Sale, but a Yard Trade) and traded most of all of his possessions for only fruits and vegetables—he wouldn't accept any money. Then Me-Tree told Jarrett that when he used to study nutrition at the university in Bellingham, Washington, he rented a piece of land for $50 a month and lived there in his tee-pee with his Border Collie dog for three years and made blueberry crepes all the time. They both took such a strong interest in each other and talked so intensely for so long that after hours of conversation, they both realized that they were still holding onto the rind of the watermelon slice that they had both eaten up hours ago when they started talking.

The next day (6/19) Jarrett, Me-Tree and You-Tree began walking into the Shenandoah National Park, Virginia.

You know how Friday, the 21st was officially the first day of summer? Well out on the trail, this day is also known as National Hike-Naked Day. So Jarrett, Me-Tree and You-Tree celebrated this day by taking off all of their clothes and only wearing a pouch, which they created with their bandanas, that supported their pee-pees. They've been calling these pouches Shlong-Shlings! They thought that more people would take part in this celebration, but it just so happens that it was only Jarrett and the two Trees, however, as they passed people on the trail, they got tons of cheers and lots of high-5's!

On the 23rd they left the Shenandoahs. All day long they were singing this one song from Joni Mitchell—*California*—but when they sang the chorus, rather than singing the word California, they would sing 'Shenandoah' instead. So the chorus went...

Shenandoah I'm coming home.
I'm going to see the folks I dig
I'll even kiss a sunset pig
Shenandoah I'm coming home.

Oh Shenandoah I'm coming home.
Oh make me feel good rock 'n roll band
I'm your biggest fan
Shenandoah, I'm coming home.

Shenandoah I'm coming home.
Oh will you take me as I am
Strung out on another (wo)man
Shenandoah I'm coming home.

Last night (6/24) they stayed at the Bears Den Hostel, which is located right on the trail, and this morning they ate blueberry pancakes that were served by a guy who's been cooking these pancakes for thru-hikers for the past 20-or so years. Jarrett said that they were deliciously perfect. The blueberries were crushed right into the batter, so all of the pancakes were purple.

Today they are going to walk 18-miles to the border of Virginia-West Virginia. They're planning on camping out on the Virginia side of the border because tomorrow (6/26) they are going to do what is called the 4-State Challenge—wake up in Virginia, hike through West Virginia (2.6-miles), hike through Maryland (40.4-miles), and then cross into Pennsylvania. This will be a total distance of 43-miles in under 24-hours—that's the challenge! They're going to make this hot energy drink in the morning, which consist of instant oatmeal, hot chocolate, instant coffee and dehydrated milk.

Once they make it to Pennsylvania, they're going to hitch a ride back down to Harpers Ferry, West Virginia, which is considered the Psychological Halfway Point of the trail. The real halfway point is about 75-miles up north in Pennsylvania. Me-Tree's brother is going to pick them up there and drive them back to his home in Washington, D.C.—there's a spectacular 4th of July fireworks show there—and on the 5th they're heading back to the trail and getting dropped off back at the Pennsylvania border.

As Jarrett was getting off the phone with me he ended the call by saying, "Shlong-shlings forever!"

He should be calling me in the next 4 days—I'll write to you all then. Hope your day is a great one :)

—Jackie

You-Tree, Me-Tree and me crossing Skyline Drive
in Shenandoah National Park
on Hike-Naked Day

DAY 73

Journal Entry—

June 26, 4-State Challenge

Filter of the mind—there wasn't any, it was turned off, released, it was opened, exposed, expressed, revealed. Back in San Luis Obispo, when I stormed out of that AmeriCorps office, the filter of my mind was broken, liberated, freed! My words were no longer held back by my thoughts, my thoughts were no longer censored by my mind, and my mind no longer repressed my feelings. My feelings blasted straight up from my heart and exploded right out of my mind. My mind couldn't hold back my heart—my heart was way too powerful—and my mind released every single emotion that I was feeling that day, with no filter, no strain, no blockage, no limit…and that was the most liberating experience of my entire life…breaking free from the filter of my mind! Me-Tree brought this awareness to me after I told him everything that had happened back in San Luis Obispo.

Early this morning (3:30am), we all woke up on the Virginia side of the border. About 20-miles later, we took a break inside of a structure on the trail in Maryland called the Washington Monument. After eating lunch for about an hour, You-Tree was ready to continue on, but Me-Tree and I decided to hold back until the storm blew over. We talked inside that structure for several hours before we continued walking again…and as we continued making our way towards Pennsylvania, I started to tell him the whole story about what had happened with my AmeriCorps program. It took me about 6-hours to explain every last detail to him, and when I was finally done, Me-Tree simply stopped in his tracks, turned around to me, gave me a huge smile, and then said, "The filter of the mind…you broke free!"

He understood. He understood and received me well…and that's all I could've ever asked for. And he was right, I broke free—free of the mind—something I had to do in order to fully release my emotions. When we break free of the mind, it is then when we are able to fully express the heart, uninterrupted by thoughts, logic, reasons and ideas, and only sponsored by emotions, passion, feelings and sentiments.

This 4-State Challenge is the most extreme thing I've ever done. I'm pushing my body to a physical extreme that it's never been pushed to before, and as a result, my mind is being pushed just as far, if not further. Not only am I experiencing an extreme journey of the body, but I'm also tapping into an even more extreme journey into the mind. I'm thinking about things I've never thought of before, feeling things I've never felt before, sensing things I've never sensed before…and Me-Tree and I are having epiphanies about things we've never realized before—epiphanies about life, death, god, religion, creation, evolution, government, education, plants, animals, time, space, the earth, the moon, the stars, and love! We're talking about it all, analyzing everything, breaking it all down, understanding it, and bringing new meaning to the whole universe—and now, it's all so clear to me, all so apparent, all so true. Everything—and I mean *everything in this universe*—is all connected, all related, all united...*all ONE!* Everything and everyone is all a part of the oneness—*the universal oneness*—the oneness that relates us all...all humans, all animals, all plants, all soil, all water, all air, all moons, all suns and all stars. It's the oneness that bonds us all together, supports us all as one, embraces us all communally, and connects us all equally. It's the oneness that we all come from. The oneness that we all belong to. The oneness that we're all a part of. And the oneness that we're all related to. And with all of my previous thoughts of truly believing that we are all a part of some spiritual union, this is the very first time in my entire life that I'm now actually *feeling* this essential oneness that I've always believed in!

Feeling this essence has been a complete opening of my mind. A full letting go of my thoughts. A total release of my mental state. It's been a mental release—a mental orgasm—an orgasm of the mind. An orgasm that's been more powerful than any other physical orgasm I've ever experienced in my entire life. Physical orgasms have only brought me closer to another body, but this mental orgasm has brought me closer to another mind...and after experiencing such an extreme mental climax with Me-Tree, we both began to wonder, "If a mental orgasm (a complete release of the mind) brings people closer together than a physical orgasm (a complete release of the body), then just imagine the possibilities of experiencing an emotional orgasm (a complete release of the heart), and then ultimately, a spiritual orgasm (a complete release of the spirit)!"

DAY 74
Journal Entry—
June 27

Me-Tree and I finished the 4-State Challenge early this morning. We saw You-Tree curled up on his Therm-A-Rest just across the Maryland-Pennsylvania border. I was so relieved to see him sleeping there that I laid down right behind him, wrapped my arm around his waist, and fell asleep by his side.

When we woke up several hours later, I called Don and Chris (the guys who live near Harpers Ferry and who gave me my trail-name) and asked them if they could offer us a ride back down south to Harpers Ferry—that's where I'm at right now. We came back down here because You-Tree's father and sister are meeting him and Me-Tree here this afternoon, and they're all driving down to the Shenandoahs to go camping for the weekend. After that, they're heading back up here to meet Me-Tree's brother who's then taking them back to his home in Washington, D.C. to celebrate the 4th of July fireworks show. Me-Tree has invited me to come along with them, so I'm spending the weekend here in town until they get back. I'm staying here at H's Place (a hostel in town), where H (the owner) bakes incredible bread and cooks delicious soup everyday.

Appalachian Trail Conference Register Entry (Harpers Ferry, West Virginia)—
6-27-02

Epiphany…Epiphany…Epiphany – The crazier my experiences are – the more in touch I become – A transition has occurred and it's time to express the transformation – Venturing into an experience which shall further put me in touch – It's about to get really crazy –

Harmony—Pacence

DAY 77
Journal Entry—
June 30

Several days ago, when I first arrived here (Harpers Ferry), H invited me to go see some live music at a local bar in town, but before we went, he said that he had to pick up two thru-hikers and bring them back to the hostel. We searched all over town for them, but couldn't find them anywhere, so before we headed off to the bar, H drove by the 7-11 as a final resort—and there they were—Jaberwoki (the girl who sang Joni Mitchell songs with You-Tree back at the YMCA campground) and her friend Hug n' Kiss. They're both hiking the trail together. I remember seeing Hug n' Kiss at the YMCA campground back in Waynesboro, Virginia, but several nights ago was the first time I really got a chance to meet her. I was sitting shotgun in H's van, my window was rolled all the way down, and she reaches her hand in and places an Echinacea thistle button on top of my right knee. She simply balances it there, looks at me, and smiles with her eyes. I smiled back. We never said a single word. We just smiled. It was a perfect way to meet.

H asked them if they wanted to go to the bar with us, so they came along. I danced to the first couple of songs by myself, shirtless, barefoot, long hair all untied—that's how I left the hostel—and then Hug n' Kiss offered me a sip of her beer by the bar. After we finished her beer, we went outside to get some fresh air. We took a short walk, sat on a stone bridge together, and then told each other about our dreams and fears. I told her that mine are one in the same. My one dream is that when I'm done hiking this trail, I'll be able to integrate all of the love that I'm finding out here back in society…and my only fear is that I won't be able to. She then shared her dreams and fears with me…and then after that…I finally asked her the awaited opening question, "What do you believe?" It may not have been the first question I had asked her, but it certainly was the first time I had asked anyone (other than You-Tree and Me-Tree) the question—and without pausing for a single moment, she simply looked right into me and said, "Love!"—that was her answer…and it was an answer that I truly connected with.

The next couple of days Hug n' Kiss and I went swimming in the confluence of the Potomac and Shenandoah rivers. I swam naked, and she said that I had a beautiful body…and beautiful hair. We also borrowed mountain bikes from H's Place and rode them around town, ate lunch together, shared a smoothie, laid on the grass, and that's when her lips finally touched mine…she kissed me. It was so beautiful…and she was so gentle.

I told her all about my epiphanies out here, all about my realizations, all about my discoveries, and then I told her how I'm going to continue hiking this trail—by simplifying my wants, only carrying my needs, and getting closer in touch with Mother Nature—and I plan on doing this by sending most of my 'wanted' gear back to Jackie and only carrying the bare essentials that I 'need'. She called me courageous…courageous! No one has ever called me that before. It was a true compliment.

Last night at H's Place, we stayed up all through night, and when the sun eventually made its way around the earth, morning light shined in through the bedroom window, and that's when we finally fell asleep together. Today, You-Tree and Me-Tree are coming back into town. I'm heading out to D.C. with them this afternoon. Hug n' Kiss will be further north on the trail when I get back. I know we'll meet up again. Thru-hikers always do.

From:	Jackie
To:	Friends & Family
Subject:	A message from Jarrett
Date:	Monday, July 1, 2002, 3:03pm

Hi everyone,

Jarrett asked me to send these new words across the world for him......

Hello everyone, to each and every one of you out there who reads about my adventures, hello. Each of you, some of you, all of you, have passed through my mind, my heart, at one step or another during my journey. I think about what you're doing, what we've been through, how life is treating you, and how you're all treating life. I hope everyone is finding happiness with each and every cycle of passing light. I miss you all, and I hope for the very best for everyone.

Transitions, epiphanies, thoughts, revelations, getting in touch, simplifying, truth, primal, changes, feelings, soul-searching...enlightenment!

It's tough to find what you're looking for when you're aware of your search!

Last week I stopped searching...and thus I found something, something deep, something real, something true, something or someone who has become reborn, awaken, aware...I found myself...in the arms of our purest mother—Mother Nature—and it was here where I found light.

It's time to embrace this transition and accept the change.

When I hiked the 4-State Challenge, I came to the profound realization that I need very little to survive with out here in nature, so I've sent everything back to my sister that I once 'wanted' for hiking the trail, and I'm only carrying the things that I now 'need' for surviving in nature. From now on, this trail is no longer about hiking, it's about surviving.

Survival—what do I need? Back when I used to work at BOCES, I used to teach a survival course that would focus on 'The Rules of 3', which talks about our basic needs for survival—air, water, food and shelter. These rules say that humans can survive:

- *3 minutes without air*
- *3 hours without shelter (in extreme weather conditions)*
- *3 days without water*
- *3 weeks without food*

Air—I have plenty of that, so I won't be needing to carry any fresh air right now...and hopefully I never will!

Shelter (which also includes clothing)—a pair of underwear, shorts, a long sleeve thin shirt, a pair of socks, and my new Chaco hiking sandals. It gets really hot and humid during the day, so I should be fine with just these clothes. For sleeping…a silk liner (used for lining the inside of a sleeping bag), a nylon hammock, which crunches down into the size of a softball, and a plastic garbage bag, which I'll stuff leaves and pine needles in for extra warmth and insulation. If it gets too cold at night, I'll either start doing jumping jacks to create my own internal heat, or I'll pack up my things and begin hiking until the sun rises and provides me with its warmth.

Water—I'll be carrying two water bottles, one that has a built-in water filter, and the other is just a regular bottle that I'll store untreated spring, stream or river water in.

Food—just fruits, vegetables, nuts and seeds—apples, bananas, oranges, carrots, cucumbers, celery, broccoli, garlic, ginger, and whatever nuts and seeds I buy in town…and when I make it into a town, that's when I'll re-supply my body with extra carbohydrates, caloric intake, protein and fat. My only disappointment with this trail has been my eating habits—Pop-Tarts, Snickers, Ramen noodles, candy bars, big cheeseburgers—and as a result, my insulin level rises and drops, rise and drops, rises and crashes. I'm also turned off at how my sweat smells because of all the preservatives and artificial nonsense I'm putting into my body. So from now on, I'm just going raw, with only eating whole organic fruits, veggies, nuts and seeds. After being out here with nature, I don't believe that I have the primal instinct to hunt…I feel like I'm more of a berry picker, not a hunter. There are others out here who are by nature, or nurture, hunters, and they do in fact hunt for their food—mostly snakes. But when I look at how my natural body is equipped—no large teeth, no long claws—I don't feel like I'm designed for hunting animals anymore. So from now on, I'm just going to eat whatever my body is capable of gathering on its own—plant food—and I feel that by just eating plant food out in nature, I'll be able to experience an even deeper connection with getting closer in touch with Mother Earth—I'll be eating her food, while drinking her water, breathing her air, and sheltering myself with her resources.

Luxury items—headlamp, toothbrush, money, a walking stick that I just picked up from a guy in town who used to grow his tobacco plants on, and my Data Book.

My backpack, tent, sleeping bag, stove, knife, compass, boots, extra clothes and hiking poles have all been sent back to Jackie. From now on, I'm only wearing the clothes I have on my back, and I'm just carrying the water bottles, raw food and luxury items I have in my new fanny pack that I just bought in town at a local gear shop.

I know this may sound crazy to most people, but I have begun to realize that the crazier society regards us, the more individually sane we feel. Or maybe that makes more sense the other way around…the more individual sane we feel, the more society regards us as crazy!

Either way, this is not about going lighter, it's not about being extreme, it's about getting in touch…in touch with Mother Nature!

I love you all, I miss you dearly, and I wish happiness and forever blissfulness to be sprinkled upon you at each and every cycle of light.

Harmony—Pacence

DAY 85
Journal Entry—
July 8

Met up with Hug n' Kiss and Jaberwoki today. It was so wonderful to see them again—especially Hug n' Kiss. You-Tree seemed just as full of wonder to see Jaberwoki. He seems to really connect with her. Amazingly enough, Hug n' Kiss and Jaberwoki just so happened to be hiking with Nappy, so I met up with him as well—what a celebration it has been—and they've all been hiking with some other thru-hiker named Smurf, the World's Traveling Redneck. He's hilarious. He's got a real thick southern accent, loves watching NASCAR, wears pink flip-flops, and has two pierced nipples and a whole collection of hand creams and sanitizing lotions in his backpack. Smurf, Nappy, Hug n' Kiss and Jaberwoki have all been hiking together for the past several days, and we just met up with them this afternoon while Smurf was lying down on the trail after getting stung in the neck by a bee. We all took really good care of him and walked him to the next shelter where he decided to stay and rest, so right now I'm continuing on with Me-Tree, You-Tree, Nappy, Hug n' Kiss and Jaberwoki, and we all just passed the halfway point on the trail. A tall wooden sign marked the point, and it read:

> **APPALACHIAN TRAIL**
> **MAINE TO GEORGIA**
> ← 1,069 SPRINGER MT. **S**
> **N** 1,069 MT. KATAHDIN →

A few miles past this sign, just outside the Pine Grove Furnace State Park, there was a little grocery store there that's known for their Half-Gallon Challenge, which is where thru-hikers attempt to eat a half-gallon of ice cream in celebration of making it to the halfway point of the trail. If a thru-hiker eats an entire half-gallon of ice cream on their own, they don't have to pay for it. I didn't attempt this challenge, but another thru-hiker did, and he didn't have to pay.

The Halfway Point

DAY 86
Journal Entry—
July 9

Me-Tree and I love walking behind Hug n' Kiss. She wears this amazing fragrant oil called Egyptian Musk that smells so incredible. He keeps saying that she's such a lover, and lately he's been calling her Love, so now that's become her new trail-name—Love. She's got the most amazing blue eyes. It's really like looking into the sky, like looking into the sea, like looking into her *self*.

Today, Love and I took our time hiking, while Me-Tree, You-Tree, Jaberwoki and Nappy pushed on ahead of us. We all agreed that we'd meet up at the next road crossing for some lunch at a nearby deli. As Love and I slowly made our way up the trail, we suddenly found ourselves getting into a really deep conversation about death. We started talking about the friends that we've both lost in our lives. I told her about my summer camp friend Jeremy Fradin who died in a car accident when he was only 16-years old, and she told me about one of her friends who had passed away at just around the same age as well. After talking for a long time about our friends that we've both lost, we finally made it the road crossing and noticed that we weren't on right trail. The entire Appalachian Trail is marked with these small white blazes (2-inch by 6-inch vertical white rectangles, which are painted at eye-level on trees and other objects in both directions to mark the official route of the trail), however we were standing at the intersection of a road crossing and a side-trail that wasn't marked with anything. I turned around and looked at all the trees behind us and there wasn't a single blaze at all. We had no idea how or when we walked off the trail, but after talking so intensely about losing our friends, we suddenly found ourselves losing our way. And then, all of a sudden, with all of the peace and understanding in Love's heart, she simply turns herself towards me, and out of the blue she says, "Pacence, we're not lost. We not lost at all. We're found. We're found by our friends. While we were talking about losing our friends, our friends were talking about finding us here…here together…here on another trail!"—and after hearing beautiful, yet simple words like that, I simply found myself rising in love with her!

From:	Jackie
To:	Friends & Family
Subject:	Last night with Pacence
Date:	Thursday, July 11, 2002, 1:57pm

Hello everyone,

I finally have a moment to put my 1-hour conversation with Pacence last night into an email. Here it goes.....

He was in D.C. for July 4th, and on the 5th and he got back on the trail (after I got off the phone with him, I realized that we didn't speak at all about his 4th—so I have no idea what the D.C. fireworks show was like). When he got back on the trail, about 2 or 3 days later, he met up with Hug n' Kiss (a girl that he met back in Harpers Ferry whose trail-name is now Love), her college friend Jaberwoki, and Nappy (the guy that Pacence saw all that bullshit with on top of the bald back in Tennessee). So now, Me-Tree, You-Tree, Nappy, Jaberwoki, Love and Pacence are all walking together and they're calling themselves 'Team Love'!

One day, while Pacence and Love were taking their time on the trail, the rest of the gang decided to meet up with them at the next road crossing at a deli. Pacence and Love got into this really deep conversation about friends and if they'd ever experienced a friend who had passed on. After having this really in-depth conversation, they finally made it to the road crossing and realized that they weren't on the Appalachian Trail. They were on some side-trail and had no clue where they were. Luckily they were able to hitch a ride back to the deli to where the rest of Team Love was, and the man that drove them there said that they had walked 8-miles off the trail and two mountains over from the AT.

On April 9th they all arrived in Boiling Springs, Pennsylvania, and Team Love decided to hitch a ride out to Love's parents home in Kennett Square, Pennsylvania. Her parents live about 3-hours away from the trail, and right now they're vacationing in Europe for the week. Team Love decided to split up into two teams and race back to Love's home by way of hitchhiking. Pacence, You-Tree and Jaberwoki were on one team, while Me-Tree, Love and Nappy were on the other. Pacence told me a very strange story about the two rides his team had hitched. They were walking along an overpass of a highway when a car drove right by them. About 30-minutes later, this same car pulls up to them and a woman asks them if they need a ride. They all get into her car and she tells them that after she passed them the first time, she kept wondering to herself whether or not she should help them out. She was contemplating this for such a long time that she eventually realized that helping them out was the right thing to do. So she drove back to pick them up and took them about an hour or so up the highway to where she had to get off. As they were all getting out of her car, she then tells them that she guarantees that their next ride will take them all the way to wherever they need to go. Well a little while later, another car pulls up to them, and this other woman (who didn't know the first woman) asks them if they need a ride. Of course they said yes and got into her car, and while this woman was driving, she basically tells them the same exact story about how she drove by them about a half an hour ago and was wondering whether or not she should help them out, and after contemplating this for such a long time, she too eventually realized that helping them out was the right thing to do. So just like the first woman, she drove back to pick them up—and exactly like the first woman said—she took them all the way to wherever they needed to go. As they were listening to this story, they were getting so freaked out. Finally, she dropped them all off, and even though it only took them just two rides to get there, the other team beat them in a total of 6 rides.

They've all been chilling at Love's parents home since the 10th (yesterday) and having a really nice time just living in a home, cooking delicious dinners and watching great movies. Last night they were getting ready for dinner at around 10:30pm—homemade pizza and a fresh salad—and they were going to watch a couple of movies—*Dumb and Dumber* and *Harold and Maude*.

They're heading back to the trail on April 12th (tomorrow). Jaberwoki's mom (who lives near Kennett Square) is driving them back to Boiling Springs, Pennsylvania to where they got off. They already passed the halfway point on the trail.

Pacence told me that he switched his nylon hammock for a colorful striped cloth Brazilian one, which comes with its own shoulder sac that he's now using instead of his fanny pack. He also said that he's now wearing a sarong (a large piece of fabric often wrapped around the waist) that he's going to bring back to the trail with him as well.

I should be hearing from Pacence in about another week or so—so until then, always remember, the 80's rock...and Michael Jackson rules!!!!!!!! (this is my personal quote)

—Jackie

—Team Love—
Pacence, Jaberwoki, Nappy, You-Tree, Love and Me-Tree
at Love's parents home

1

Journal Entry—
July 14

Made it to Duncannon, Pennsylvania. Stayin' here at the Doyle Hotel. Nappy's foot is a bit sore and he's having a really hard time walking on it, so he's decided to stay back and rest here for awhile.

Several nights ago, Me-Tree, Love and I were talking about different ways to distribute the weight of our gear. Our conversation was inspired by seeing someone strap their tent poles to their hiking poles with duct tape. Me-Tree started thinking about the possibilities of rather than strapping his gear to the outside of his poles, what about stuffing it inside of them. So when he made it to the next town, he bought himself two 5-foot thick PVC pipes with plastic stoppers on each end and constructed these enormous hiking poles that now carries all of his gear. His silk liner, nylon hammock, Cliff bars (energy bars) and all his other food are stuffed right inside these massive poles, and now he's only carrying the weight of his water on his back in his new hydration backpack.

Last night I met Trail-Angel Mary—Duncannon's renowned trail-angel—and today she gave me a white and orange striped beach bag so that I can carry more food in—extra vegetables, hummus and fresh baked bread. We ate breakfast at her home this morning, and then later in the afternoon, a man in town, who calls himself Sedentary Steve, interviewed me for his book that he's writing about the AT. He's interviewing as many thru-hikers as he can who passes through this town. He took a picture of me and said that he'll email a copy of the photo and the interview to me sometime tomorrow.

From:	Jackie
To:	Friends & Family
Subject:	Fwd: AT Interview & Photo
Date:	Monday, July 15, 2002, 2:00pm
Attachment:	Pacence (July 14)

Hello everyone,

Here's an email from a man that interviewed Pacence for his book on the AT. He's included an attached photo, which was taken of Pacence in Duncannon, Pennsylvania. Pacence is now walking with just the two bags that are in the picture. In them—his hammock, water bottles, vegetables and bread. Pretty righteous living he says!

—Jackie

Hi Pacence,

Thanks for the interview in Duncannon on July 14. Here's a copy of our interesting interview from the gutter outside the Doyle. The attached jpg. was snapped just across the street.

—Sedentary Steve

Where's your home, Pacence?

"Earth. I used to build up walls to protect myself. Now I'm shedding these walls and breaking them down to get to the essence of myself, which I'm learning is love. I'm falling in love with myself out here, and that allows me to love everything and everyone I surround myself with."

Why did you decide to hike the AT, Pacence?

"After experiencing Corporate America and a nonprofit organization that disappointed me, I was searching for something that I could do day in and day out that was 100 percent honest and pure. And that I am in complete control of. A place for myself that I could experience absolute freedom. I found it on the trail. I'm living based on impulse—if you're hungry, you eat. I've never been so selfish (living a life in a way that brings total happiness) *and it's bringing me harmony in everything I do. I'm giving 100 percent of myself and not catering to external expectations."*

Where did you go to school, Pacence?

"*I started as a Film major at the University of Buffalo. Then I did a semester abroad in Seville, Spain. In 1999, I graduated from Hofstra University with a major in Film and a minor in Biology.*"

Do you carry a camera?

"*Yes, I carry a camera for my sister. I send her a roll of film every week.*"

Pacence, what's your take on the number of females on the AT?

"*There's a skewed ratio—a low percentage. On the trail a lot of males are getting in touch with their feminine side and females are in touch with their masculine side. The gender roles that we're conditioned to live with slowly fizzles away on the trail. The same with nationality, race and age. All these notions were created by society. But out here in nature, we're all just simple humans walking the earth and satisfying our basic needs.*"

Attachment: Pacence (July 14)

DAY 95
Journal Entry—
July 18

Made it to Port Clinton, Pennsylvania. Been walking with Love through the night. We've been talking about wanting to live on a farm together, living simply, raising chickens and cows, growing an organic garden and living in a peaceful home. We're both really coming together on this. We're completely connecting with one another out here. And we're totally rising in love with each other!

She's so simple, so real, so natural, grows hair where it's supposed to, doesn't care, but cares so much. Cares so much about love. Believes in it wholeheartedly. Sometimes when I walk behind her, she stops on the trail, turns around to me, closes her eyes, presses her lips together and says, "Kiss it!" Other times she takes my hand, leads me into the forest, and makes love to me. To be taken by the hand, led into nature and rise in love with someone is the ultimate experience. Her love pulls the blood of my body like the moon pulls the water of this earth. She's like a goddess out here...like a goddess of the woods. I could spend my entire life with this woman...and she feels the same way about me. Our love is so pure, so innocent, so honest, so simple. Love is so simple out here in nature. There are no outside influences, no external pressures, no restrictions, no stress— just love—just pure simple love. The love inside us all. The love inside of you. The love inside of me. The love inside of her. *The love inside us all...that's it!*

I'm essentially being *the love inside us all* and getting in touch with my true self out here. I'm communicating with myself and finally acting. I'm making one with myself. Expressing myself. Not being afraid of myself. Hearing what myself is telling my outer to do and doing it. Listening to myself and doing. Making one with myself. Connecting my inner self with my outer self. Simply getting in touch. Knowing myself!!! Letting myself be known. Loving myself. Coming out and loving all. I'm coming out!

My love is coming out now that I've completely broken myself down, fully stripped myself apart, totally exposed myself...that's where I found my love, my purest, most real emotion...love. That's where it existed. That's how I found it. Love. True love...*me* connecting with *you*...the *me* in me loving the *you* in you. She loves the *me* she feels, not the me she sees. Yes! Yes, yes, yes! It's so easy...so easy to come out, so easy to bring *me* out.

The *me* that was once so fragile and had to be handled with absolute care...the *me* that might never have come out in my entire life, but it did...it did for this one shining moment of final revelation, and now I feel most alive, most known, most understood, most real. The *me* that I once buried so deeply within my outer self of myself came out...my *me* that was so hidden from my society, my friends, family, my loved ones, and even my own self...the *me* that was so boarded up and stored away and protected. And now that I've fully broken myself apart, now that I've cracked myself wide open, it is here, and it is now, when my true colors shine, my true intentions, my true feelings, my true emotions, my purest strength…my purest, truest, most real me…the *me* inside me. When I completely broke myself down, I found my…my inner strength!

DAY 99
Journal Entry—
July 22

Delaware Water Gap, Pennsylvania—0.2-miles south of the New Jersey border. Love is leaving the trail tomorrow. She ran out of money and her parents are picking her up in the morning. We all offered to help her out, but she just couldn't accept our offer, and besides, she's planning on going to law school next year and has to start studying for the LSAT exams. It's going to be really sad to see her go tomorrow. She brought so much love to our trail-family. Tomorrow...Me-Tree, You-Tree, Jaberwoki and I will continue hiking north without Love's body by our side, but with her mind, heart and soul within us all.

DAY 100
Journal Entry—
July 23

~ LOVE ~
Blue jay...oh pretty blue jay, how you once flew...
with such ease, such delight, such grace ~
here ~ there ~ everywhere.
You flew...and lived...
and breathed.
And danced in the air ~ blue jay.
Oh beautiful blue jay ~ how you once danced.

Blue jay...why did it end today ~ or why a new beginning,
for you.
For you lay there...quiet, still, resting on your chest, for a time ~
no, for an experience, that brings light to new beginnings,
new lessons,
new awareness.
Oh blue jay...you rest so peacefully, in such comfort,
as you await your new journey, your new flight.
You move onward, with the past behind,
the future unexpected,
and the present cherished.
Blue jay...oh blue jay ~ I learn from our intersection.
Oh pretty blue...thank you.

~ Pacence

DAY 101
Journal Entry—
July 24

What a great surprise! Jackie visited me on the trail today and surprised me with mom and dad. It's so great to see them again. Being back with my family always makes me realize how much I miss them when I'm away. It's nice not to miss them right now.

From:	Jackie
To:	Friends & Family
Subject:	Pacence at his best
Date:	Wednesday, July 31, 2002, 1:34pm

Hi everyone,

Quickly I had the chance to speak to Pacence today. He is in Bear Mountain, New York. Can you guys believe it? Connecticut, Massachusetts, Vermont, New Hampshire and then Maine—I can't believe he is almost done with the trail. I asked him what he's going to do once he makes it to Maine and he said, sort of jokingly, "Walk back to Georgia." He's with Me-Tree right now, and You-Tree and Jaberwoki are 2-days ahead of them. Poetry In Motion (another thru-hiker that they met on the trail from Ohio) is ahead of them as well, but only 1-day. Last night Pacence camped out on Bear Mountain in his Hammy (that's his hammock's trail-name) overlooking New York City—such a trip. He started screaming on top of the mountain to all of his New York friends—I guess he was a tad bit excited. Tomorrow the trail goes right through the Bear Mountain Zoo. In three days he will be in Connecticut. The funniest thing he said to me today was that all the way from Georgia to New Jersey he never fell once, but as soon as he crossed into New York (his home state) he fell down twice (nothing bad happened to him), and one night he was looking down at the ground while he was walking and he walked right into a branch of a tree. Me-Tree was laughing so hard, and when Pacence finally realized what had happened to him, he started laughing as well.

Other than that, he is doing great and will be contacting friends that emailed me about meeting up with him on the trail.

Hope everyone is doing gr-8 :)

—Jackie

On top of Bear Mountain

DAY 112
Riga Lean-to Register Entry—
8-4

I love nature! QWA (Me-tree's trail-nickname)→pushed onto next shelter (1-mile). Hopefully You-Tree and Jab's are there. See you soon.

Harmony—Pacence

From:	Jackie
To:	Friends & Family
Subject:	Hey
Date:	Wednesday, August 7, 2002, 10:45pm

Hi everyone,

Here's a quick email from Pacence. Hope everyone is doing well.

Hello to all. It's been awhile since I've checked my messages and replied. I want you all to know how important it has been for me to hear all of your responses and sincere interest in my travels. I am looking forward to the New England portion of the trail and then reuniting with you all to share experiences and stories.

I'm in Massachusetts right now! This Friday I'll be crossing into Vermont. I have another 600-or so miles to go—just walked 1500-miles! Whew!

Everything is changing, once again—people, climate, vegetation, food, towns, amount of sunlight, animals, hills, mountains, rivers, lakes, awareness, purposes, goals, ME!

You-Tree, Jaberwoki and I just drank several cold Snapple ice teas in town, and underneath the caps were these trivia facts:

- *Only bird to fly backwards—hummingbird*
- *Only food that doesn't spoil—honey*
- *Number of grooves on the edge of a quarter—119*

Everything is everything.

Harmony—Pacence

From:	Jackie
To:	Friends & Family
Subject:	Email message
Date:	Saturday, August 10, 2002, 4:47pm

Hi everyone,

Here's another message from Pacence. Enjoy.

Slowin' down—not movin' so fast—just makin' the moment last…
Kickin' down the cobblestone—lookin' for fun and feelin' groovy!

Got no deeds to do—no promises to keep…
I'm dappled and drowsy and ready for sleep…
Lettin' the morning time drop all its petals on me…
Life I love you—all is groovy!

Language is extremely limiting and restrictive when trying to describe my state of being right now. But there is one phrase that pretty much sums up where I'm at these days…*life I love you, all is groovy!*

I have fallen in love with myself out here, and with life…and with this, comes everything! I love everything and everyone, and for the first time in my life, I am truly experiencing what it means to feel. Feeling without the filtration of the mind. Just a constant state of exploding emotions. Life is pretty powerful right now, and I'm riding this wave out to the very end!

This trail has taken on many transitions. In the beginning it was all physical…my physical body and the physical trail working harmoniously together to push onward. Then the trail took a turn…it turned right into my mind…and it had nothing to do with the physical aspect of hiking anymore…it was all mental. As I continued walking the trail, my mind entered a pilgrimage of thoughts and ideas, concerns and worries, challenges and struggles, knowledge and lessons. Next came the emotional trail…and it was here where I felt completely and totally connected to this experience. A relationship, an intimate relationship, had developed between the journey and myself. And now, the most recent transition has occurred…a shift from all these levels and stages towards the one final state of enlightenment…and this is what it has most recently become…a trail of life, the Life Trail, the LT! It's not physical/mental/emotional/spiritual anymore…there exists no separation between these levels any longer…it has all merged into one harmonious awareness—love!

So as limiting as I claim language to be in explaining experiences like this one…this is the best way I can clearly articulate where I'm at right now.

The most recent lesson I have learned on the trail has been:

> *You don't have to be on the trail…to be on The Trail!*

Love to all.

Be kind and gentle with everything you handle and everyone you touch, and give thanks…much thanks to all!

Harmony—Pacence

From:	Jackie
To:	Friends & Family
Subject:	Pacence
Date:	Friday, August 16, 2002, 9:53am

Hi everyone,

I just got a call from Pacence. He and Me-Tree hitched a ride out to Ohio several days ago to pick up Me-Tree's Toyota pickup truck at his cousin's place. Me-Tree wanted to drive his truck up to Maine and park it somewhere so that he'll have it when he's done with the trail. On their way up to Maine, Me-Tree dropped Pacence off at Love's home in Pennsylvania. Pacence is planning on staying there for a week and then meeting back up with Me-Tree, You-Tree and Jaberwoki in Hanover, New Hampshire on the 23rd. I asked him if he was going to hitch a ride up there or walk from Pennsylvania again???

The big news is that Pacence cut off all of his hair. His hair is now only 1-inch long!!!!! Can you believe it? He's had long hair for years. I can't wait to see a picture of him!

Have a great weekend :)

—Jackie

From:	Jackie
To:	Friends & Family
Subject:	Words can't explain how amazing this email is—enjoy:)
Date:	Saturday, August 24, 2002, 9:22pm

Hi everyone,

Here's another message from Pacence. Enjoy!

Hanover, New Hampshire…400-and some odd miles to go until I reach my final climb…Mount Katahdin! We've walked about 1700-miles and we're not about to stop now. We're dedicated, passionate, committed, determined, and strong…all great lessons in life…if you're involved in something you truly believe in.

Life has been, and continues to be lovely!

In a couple of days from now I'll be heading into the great White Mountains of New Hampshire. Those mountains are known to have the most severe weather conditions on earth. WIND CITY! Population=whoever dares to hike through them! It's been recorded that wind speeds have reached up to 200+miles per hour. People have been known to have been blown right off the mountains. Proceeding with caution.

Jackie has sent back some of my warm gear for the last leg of the hike—backpack, tent, sleeping bag, a fleece shirt and pair of lightweight pants. With the weather getting cooler, my gear has gotten warmer. Receiving these items really put into perspective how long I have been out here for. I started in Georgia on April 15th…early spring, 57-pounds of what I thought was simplifying my life into a backpack, it was cold, rainy, sometimes snowy, big uphill battles, painful downhill struggles, crossing my first border…North Carolina, very emotional, a huge achievement, however 12-states still lie in the distance…then came the Smoky Mountains, encounters with bears, blooming flowers, songs of morning birds, surrounded by nature, made it to Hot Springs, a job offer to work on a farm and build a eco-friendly home, Trail Days, hitchhiking, crossing the Tennessee border, hurting knees, burning blisters, sore feet, aching back, filtering water, eating dehydrated soup, hiking with Katu, meeting Nappy, night-hiking, crossing into Damascus, Virginia…my first real big goal, meeting Me-Tree and You-Tree, hiking the Shenandoah Mountains, spotting deer, raccoons, squirrels, chipmunks, skunks, bobcats, owls, and hearing howling coyotes in the evening distance, Hike-Naked Day, campfires, shelters, breaking down my tent, setting it up again, breaking it down, setting it up again, hiking the 4-State Challenge in 24-hours…that's 43-miles!!!, epiphanies, realizations, awareness, getting in touch with something but not being able to identify with it, what's happening, things feel different, look different, seem different, viewing life from a different angle, a different perspective, a different point of view, feeling, feeling, feeling, stop thinking, feeling, I realize why I am out here, what this is all about, what's really important for me and in life, what I need to survive, not to hike but to survive…I hitch back down to Harpers Ferry, West Virginia, send everything back that I once wanted and keep only the things that I need, I become simplified, lighter, more fluid in my actions, in my movements, in my thoughts, in my heart, in my soul…I meet Jaberwoki and Hug n' Kiss, 4th of July in Washington, D.C., cross the halfway point in Pennsylvania, hitchhiking 300-miles to Love's home in Kennett Square, making dinners, renting movies, *Harold and Maude*, Team Love, back on the trail, birds, wind, trees, mountains, air, sunrises, sunsets, hikers, smiling faces everywhere, love, life, rising in love, rising in life, the search is over, I've stopped searching, stopped thinking, stopped asking, stopped questioning, stopped trying to figure it all out, and then BANG!…it hits me like a ton of bricks…as soon as I stop, as soon as I turn off my mind, as soon I stop the filtration of thoughts, I begin to act impulsively, I begin to satisfy my needs, my desires, my wants, my wishes, I become satisfied, I'm directed by my heart and what I feel, the separation between my inner self and my outer self minimizes until there exists no space at all, I become one, I become whole, I become me, I become one with everything…with me, with you, with him, with her, with the trail, with the trees, with the birds, the water, the air, the fire, the earth, the stars, with everything, with life, and I shine, and I begin to live, I begin to love, and for the first time in my life I am truly living, truly feeling, truly being, truly loving…and I hike, and I eat, and I drink, and I sleep, and I hike, all the way into New Jersey, Bear Mountain, New York, Connecticut, Massachusetts, Vermont, and then one evening I wake up in my hammock to a light shining down on me and I'm answering "Yes, yes, yes!" in my sleep, and it's Me-Tree with his headlamp on asking me if I want to go to Ohio with him to pick up his pickup truck so we can have it up in Maine for when we're done with the trail…so the next morning we hitch out to Ohio, drive to Love's home, Me-tree drops me off, I spend several days with her, eat, drink, and lounge, she cuts all my hair off, shaves my beard, I undergo an enormous physical change, which allows me to realize that I've been holding onto my hair for reasons due to insecurities, but when it's all cut off, I feel completely unaffected by the change, which further confirms my epiphanies about our physical world…and now, here I am, back with You-Tree, Me-Tree and Jaberwoki, in Hanover, New Hampshire, in this library, on this computer, and only 400-some odd miles away from Mount Katahdin and I'm about to hike through the White Mountains, a place where hikers go to train who are planning to summit Mount Everest because of its incredibly severe weather conditions, and after sitting here and reflecting on my experiences hiking the trail up to this point, I am left here with only one thing on my mind right now…my short hair!

I love you all—wish me luck, and send me prayers and blessings—this chapter is almost over!

And soon the page will turn, and a whole new book awaits!

Harmony to all, be kind to everyone and be gentle with everything you do—because the other person is you!

Harmony—love—Pacence

DAY 142
Journal Entry—
September 3
<u>Take a Little Time</u>
Take a little time,
  A little time…to unwind,
     …to find.
I'm takin' a little time,
  A little time…for my mind.

And you'll feel what you what from life.
And you'll feel what you need to survive.
And you'll feel what you love to do.
And you'll feel what's in love with you.

Take a little time,
  A little time…to unwind,
     …to find.
I'm takin' a little time,
  A little time…for my mind.

Doesn't have to be a decade,
  Or even a year.
Not a half a year,
  Or even a month.
Doesn't have to be a half a month,
  Or even a week.
  Not even a day,
  Or even an hour.

Just right here, right now,
Just for this song—
  It won't take long.

DAY 143
Journal Entry—
September 4

Mount Washington—elevation 6,288-feet! Wow…I can't believe how powerful the wind is blowing up here. It's going to be quite a challenge walking through this wind along the Presidential Range (the mountain range located in the White Mountains).

I just read a long wooden sign propped up by two thick wooden stumps on top of Mount Washington that said:

THE NORTHERN PEAKS OF THE PRESIDENTIAL RANGE
MT. WASHINGTON STATE PARK ELEVATION—6,288
THE APPALACHIANS

The Appalachians are among the oldest mountains on earth reaching back more than 500 million years into time. The President Chain which stretches from the gaspe to Georgia once may have been higher than the Alps or the Rocky Mountains. Weather and erosion have sculptured the mountains and left them as they are today. They provide a wonderful richness of plant and animal life as well as startling contrasts in mountain scenery as different as the White Mountain National Forest and the Great Smoky National Park. Along the crest of the Appalachian Mountains, a footpath extends 2,202 miles from Mt. Katahdin 5,267' in Maine to Springer Mountain 3,782' in Georgia.

NH DIVISION OF PARKS & RECREATION

The Northern Peaks of the Presidential Range

DAY 145
Journal Entry—
September 6

Gorham, New Hampshire—just left the Whites. Me-tree and I ran into Nappy this afternoon in town. It was so great to see him again, but he was feeling really distressed by what had just happened up on Mount Washington. An older man—a thru-hiker—was found up there. Nappy was hiking with him just before this man decided to climb up Mount Washington on his own. The weather was pretty stormy on the day he climbed, and Nappy feels somewhat responsible for not stopping him. Nappy was on his way to meet up with some other thru-hikers who also walked with this man to grieve this terrible loss. How awful. I can't believe a thru-hiker just died up there.

From:	Jackie
To:	Friends & Family
Subject:	The Third Path
Date:	Monday, September 9, 2002, 4:45pm

Here's another email from Pacence…

The forces of the universe harmonize once again.

I was hitchhiking about 100-miles south of here, here is Gorham, New Hampshire, and this kind woman picked up You-Tree, Jaberwoki and I, and drove us back to the trail after we ate breakfast at a little restaurant. Me-Tree was ahead of us at the time. Now we're all together again in Gorham, just had an amazing Indian dining experience, and this same woman who picked us up about 100-miles south of here was sitting in the restaurant. She calls out my name, we talk, and now I'm spending the night at her beautiful home with Me-Tree and Sarah. Sarah is a friend that we met along the way in the White Mountains. She teaches environmental education up there and had some time off. You-Tree and Jaberwoki decided to continue on.

The Whites have been a blast. Mount Washington, ridge walking above tree line, staying at the huts (lodges that have been provided by the Appalachian Mountain Club for backpackers to stay overnight), working for stay—doing dishes, stacking wood, performing skits for their guests, holding a 2-hour question and answer discussion with the hut guests about our experiences thru-hiking the trail—all in exchange for staying at these beautiful huts nestled in the White Mountains, eating the most cared-for and loved-for food—soups, fresh baked bread, lasagna, salads, pumpkin pies, vegetables, blueberry pancakes, juices, hot cocoa, and just good wholesome righteous food. We really took our time hiking through those Whites, averaging about 5-6 miles a day, jumping from hut to hut…but just because we were only hiking 5-6 miles a day doesn't mean we were taking it easy. Those mountains kicked our ass! Straight uphill 5000-feet, straight downhill 4000-feet, straight up 6000-feet, straight down 5000-feet, and so on and so forth, with howling winds blowing up to 75-miles per hour per day. Blew me right down several times. We had to walk bent down into the wind. I've never screamed so loud and for so long in my life. We all were. We kept screaming into that wind, "What's the big hurry, slow down, you'll get there!"—but there was no mercy. It was like the louder we screamed, the harder the wind blew. Powerful! Despite the battle though, walking above tree line has been both miraculous and beautiful, inspiring and wonderful.

For the past 5-months, I've been walking through what's been referred to as 'The Green Tunnel'. The entire Appalachian Trail, except for the part that goes through the Whites, is known for its continuous green canopy. So it was really nice to finally be exposed to all the elements of what lies above the trees. This type of vast exposure has allowed for different kinds of expansive thoughts, being embraced in such a wide-open setting. It has given room for my soul to explore different paths in a direct relationship to these wide-open spaces. While hiking the Whites, some inspiring words were needing to come out about paths, and life, and struggles, and choices, and direction. At one time in my life, not too long ago, I wrote down similar words for a friend who was struggling with life's decisions. This time it was me up there...struggling...and with these following words, I found a new peace for my new struggle:

—*The Third Path*—

As we wander up the path of our lives, we are constantly being exposed to the many changes of terrain. With each change, our stride is directly affected.

Sometimes, we encounter a terrain of a smooth and well-maintained nature, and so we walk our path with ease and total comfort.

Sometimes the terrain we encounter is rocky and irregular and we often find ourselves stumbling and losing our footing.

Often times we are exposed to a terrain that will take us straight uphill and so we are faced with a challenge and much hard work.

And often times our terrain will take us straight downhill where we may ache a bit, however here, we are usually able to catch our breath.

Lastly, we experience a terrain unlike no other, and it's this particular terrain that usually stops us in our stride, for we must now ponder our path. Here, we are faced with a choice, a decision, an option, and we must choose wisely, for here, our path splits into two.

The Mind's Path:

The first of these two paths bends slightly to the right and then continues straight ahead. This path is often referred to as The Mind's Path. If taken, you will be satisfying your thoughts, your wants, your reasons, your logic, your wonders, your curiosities, your knowledge, your brain, your mind.

Success will always be achieved here if one is truly in touch with one's mental well-being. Your mind will be satisfied, your intellect challenged, and your thoughts cleared. Mental awareness is achieved!

The Heart's Path:

The second of these two paths bends slightly to the left and then continues straight ahead adjacent to The Mind's Path. This path is often referred to as The Heart's Path. If taken, you will be satisfying your feelings, your needs, your desires, your emotions, your dreams, your lust, your passions, your heart.

Success will always be achieved here if one is truly in touch with one's emotional well-being. Your heart will be satisfied, your dreams will come true, and your passions fulfilled. Emotional awareness is achieved!

The Third Path:

The third of these two paths is a path that is only explored by the soul within. For the soul within is able to see, hear, smell, taste, touch, and feel its way onto this third path. The soul is the true connection between one's mind and one's heart. And so it holds the hidden truth to this wondrous path. The soul within will place a right foot on The Mind's Path and a left foot on The Heart's Path and begin walking forward. This creates a path that is known as The Third Path. If taken, you will be satisfying both your thoughts and your feelings, both your wants and your needs, both your reasons and your desires, both your logic and your emotions, both your wonders and your lust, both your curiosities and your passions, both your knowledge and your dreams, and both your mind and your heart.

Success will always be achieved here, for one is truly in touch with both one's mind and one's heart. Mental awareness achieved, emotional awareness achieved, soul satisfied!

I wish for us all to always choose our paths wisely, and forever find harmony with the terrain that lies ahead.

Peace—love—harmony—Pacence

DAY 149
Journal Entry—
September 10

I just got my first taste of how trail-love is misunderstood back in society.

Took a 0-day in Gorham, New Hampshire. Touristy little town. A Main Street with lots of attractions. A couple hours ago, Me-Tree and I were walking around town with our headlamps on and sarongs tied around our waists. It was late, and all the stores were getting ready to close up for the night. We passed this one store, a touristy store, that sold all sorts of sweatshirts and hats and banners that said *'Gorham, New Hampshire'* on it. There was this one girl vacuuming the front of the store. She was the only worker there. We walked in and asked her if she needed some help. Me-tree offered to vacuum so that she could finish doing other things. She smiled, handed over the vacuum, and then started counting money behind the register. While Me-Tree was busy vacuuming the front mat of the store, I asked her if she could use some help behind the register. She said no, so I decided to straighten up around the store…and then all of a sudden, I saw her crying while she was talking on the phone. I walked over to Me-Tree and told him to look, and when she hung up the phone, we asked her what was the matter. She said something about her boyfriend just breaking up with her, and she continued to cry. Me-Tree and I tried to make her smile by putting on these huge foam animal hats—I wore an elephant on my head while he wore a parrot—but that only made her cry more. We felt so bad, so sorry, we were only trying to make her feel better, but instead we were making her feel worse, so we put the hats back on the shelf, and at that moment, a woman comes running into the store, darts behind the register, holds the girls tightly, and consoles her for a moment. Then out of nowhere, she points at Me-Tree and I and tells us to get out of the store! What? Why? What happened? What did we did wrong? Why were we getting kicked out of the store? We were so confused. We were only trying to help. Only trying to make her feel better. Why was that woman so mad at us? And who was that woman anyway?

Without asking any of these questions, we quietly left the store and started making our way down the street, and after a couple of blocks of wondering what had happened, we finally figured it out. Me-Tree was vacuuming the front of the store, which probably appeared as if he was blocking the front entrance, and when I asked her if she could use some help behind the register, that's when she made the phone call and started crying. She probably thought we were going to rob her! She must've called that woman and told her that we were going to rob the store! Oh no…what a misunderstanding! What a terrible misunderstanding! If that's what she really thought, what a huge mistake. We had to tell her the truth…we had to straighten it out. We couldn't let that girl continue working in that store with that thought in mind, with that memory in mind, with that fear in mind.

So we walked back to the store, the doors were locked, so we knocked on the front window and motioned to the woman that we really wanted to talk to her, and all she did was point to us and then point down the street, motioning to us that we should get the hell out of there. We couldn't believe it…we were right! She really thought we were trying to rob the store! What a mess. What a horrible mess. We were only trying to help. Only trying to offer our love. Only trying to give something back after receiving so much from the trail…and our offer was being totally misunderstood!

We had to do something, something more, something else. So we wrote a letter, explaining everything, and when we walked back to the store to slip it under the door, there was a police car parked out in front. What! We couldn't believe it. This was getting worse and worse by the moment, but still, we were so determined to offer our explanation and receive their understanding. So we walked over to the police car, explained everything to the officer that was standing outside of the store…and we handed the letter over to him as well. We told him that we didn't want that girl to get freaked out every time a couple of thru-hikers walked into her store late at night, and after telling him the whole story, the police officer, who was so kind and wonderfully understanding, simply looked at us and said, "Don't worry fellas, this is the third time we've received a call from this girl ever since she's worked here. It's not you, she just gets a bit scared sometimes when she closes up the store. But ya know what, with the way you two are dressed up right now with your headlamps on, I don't blame her, so why don't you get yourselves back to the trail and I'll explain everything to them inside."

Wow…what a mix-up. What a mistake. What a terrible misunderstanding. Could that really have been my first taste of how trail-love is going to be misunderstood back in society?

From:	Jackie
To:	Friends & Family
Subject:	My final ascent
Date:	Sunday, September 15, 2002, 8:17pm

This email from Pacence ROCKS!!!!!!

Well, it's September 15th…I am celebrating my 5th month anniversary of hiking the Appalachian Trail. 5-months ago, I was heading into the wilderness, unknowing of what to expect from my journey, scared, confused, confident, strong, weak, nervous, ill-prepared. I was leaving civilization and society as I knew it, to venture off to an environment and community with a new set of standards, a new set of norms, a new set of ideas and beliefs and a new way of living and appreciating life. I was setting off to be with and to live in harmony with Mother Earth, and I had no idea what was in store for me. I was a child journeying off into an earth where I had no idea where I belonged, where I existed, where I fit in, where I was…and now, 5-months later…here I sit, after what has been the most profound maturing experience of my life, and I'm ready to climb my final mountain, not as a scared child, not a nervous boy, not as an inexperienced, confused, out-of-touch adult, but as a loved man, a man who knows love, who understands love, and who has experienced the most purest form of love…self-love.

I am about to head into the final stretch of the Appalachian Trail. It's called the 100-Mile Wilderness. It's the final challenge that stands in the way between me and Mount Katahdin. It's the longest stretch of the trail that does not cross a single road, does not have a single sign, no homes, no stores, no post offices, no places to re-supply food, no hostels, NO PEOPLE! From Monson, Maine, I enter this 100-Mile Wilderness stretch after passing a warning sign to all hikers. "BE PREPARED!"—it reads. And it warns you to have enough food to make it through! Once completed, there she will be, the beautiful, the magical, the wonderful Mount Katahdin…the mountain that I have been walking towards for the past 5-months…there it will be, and there I will be. In about a week from today, my body would have walked all the way from Springer Mountain, Georgia on April 15th to Mount Katahdin, Maine on September ??, my mind would have journeyed from the darkest depths of one's imagination to the brightest clearest thoughts of one's mind, my heart would have experienced the most painful, heart-retching emotions to the greatest, most wondrous love known to life, and my soul…my soul would have begun a search from a lost place within the existence of humankind to a found place that is free to run and fly with all dreams and impulses known to life…in a about a week from today, I would have traveled from a boy to a MAN!

I have saved all of the email messages and thoughts and words that you have all written to me and me to you…and I'd just like to share one of our very first messages to each other. It's amazing how far we've come!

From:	Jackie
To:	Friends & Family
Subject:	Jarrett's first day on the trail
Date:	Monday, April 15, 2002, 2:50pm

Hi everyone,

YES!!!! I finally got a call from Jarrett today and he's psyched. He took a 13½-hour bus ride from Washington, D.C. to Gainesville, Georgia. On the bus he met two guys who are also hiking the AT—Trevor from Pennsylvania, and Greg from Massachusetts. Once they arrived in Gainesville, they all took a cab up to Amicalola State Park—$75.00 cab ride!! When they got to the park, Jarrett weighed his backpack at a whooping 57-pounds—most of this weight is the food he brought along with him and the water he's carrying, but he did tell me that without this food and water, the weight of his pack is still 35-pounds on his back—UHG!!!

Anyway, he just signed in at the visitor's center as an Appalachian Trail thru-hiker and today he's hiking 8.8-miles on the Approach Trail to get to the top of Springer Mountain—that's where the Appalachian Trail begins. The weather down there is gorgeous. The sun is out, the trees are looking happy, and he's freaking walking to MAINE!!!!! Oh, I just went to the post office and mailed him his food for the next two mail drops that he'll be stopping at.

I'll keep in touch—Jackie

Crazy isn't it!

Jackie, I love you so much, more than these words can ever describe. If it weren't for you, this journey would not have been possible. Thank you so much for all your love and support. And you know what…it took me 5-months to finally realize something that you've always said that is so incredibly true…the 80's do rock! And yes, Michael Jackson does rule! Thanks sis…you're the best!

And to all of you out there who have been with me throughout my travels…thank you all from the bottom and top of my entire being for sticking it out with me and believing that what I once thought was impossible, is in fact possible. I love you all and I'm looking forward to being with you all sometime soon.

Peace—love—harmony—Pacence

DAY 155
Journal Entry—
September 16

Here we go. The 100-Mile Wilderness. Just passed the warning sign. It read:

> # CAUTION
> THERE ARE NO PLACES TO OBTAIN
> SUPPLIES OR HELP UNTIL YOU REACH
> ABOL BRIDGE—90 MILES NORTH.
> YOU SHOULD NOT ATTEMPT THIS SECTION
> UNLESS YOU CARRY A MINIMUM OF TEN
> DAYS' SUPPLIES. DO NOT UNDERESTIMATE
> THE DIFFICULTY OF THIS SECTION.
> GOOD HIKING!
>
> M.A.T.C.

DAY 160
Hurd Brook Lean-to Register Entry—
9-21

Six months ago, I couldn't find the words to explain to my family and friends why I was going to hike the AT. 6-months later, I still can't find those words. Back then, I didn't know how to explain why I needed to do this, I just knew I needed to. And now, I still don't know how to explain why I needed to do this, I just know. Sometimes in life, we can't find the words to describe our dreams, our passions, our needs. So rather than talking about it…we simply live it. I may not have the words to describe what happened to me out here, and I may never have those words, but I do have one thing that I will keep with me forever in life—I have the experience—and with that, I have the smiles, the hugs, the friendships, and the entire thru-hiking community. I have the knowledge, the awareness, the realizations, and all the epiphanies I became aware of out here. I have the thoughts, the feelings, the emotions, and all the love I've received from this beautiful Earth. And most of all, I have something that I will truly keep with me for the rest of my life—I have me, myself, my life, and all my love I now have to offer this wonderful world!

This has truly been an experience of a lifetime, and I'd like to express my deepest appreciation to this entire Appalachian Trail.

Thanks to all the sunrises, all the morning birds, all the uphills, and all the views.

Thanks to all the roots, all the rocks, all the flowers, and all the trees.

Thanks to all the ants, all the deer, all the bears, and all the hawks.

Thanks to all the springs, all the creeks, all the streams, and all the rivers.

Thanks to all the trail-names, all the trail-towns, all the trail-magic, and all the trail-angels.

Thanks to all the snow, all the rain, all the fog, and all the sun.

Thanks to all the fire-pits, all the privies, all the registers, and all the shelters.

Thanks to all the thru-hikers, all the section-hikers, all the day-hikers, and the entire Appalachian Trail community.

Thanks to all the steps, all the ladders, all the bridges, and all the overpasses.

Thanks to all the soil, all the water, all the fire, and all the wind.

Thanks to the Appalachian Trail Conference, all its members, all its volunteers, and all its hard work.

Thanks to all the farms, all the meadows, all the valleys, and all the mountain-tops.

Thanks to all the scenery, all the downhills, all the evening crickets, and all the sunsets.

Thanks to the moon, the sun, the stars, and the universe.

Thanks to this entire wild and natural Earth!

Thank you for your spring, your summer, your fall, and your soon to be winter. Thank you Appalachian Trail.

Thank you for your continuous footpath, your white blazes, your dedicated direction, and your committed guidance.

And of course, for walking along with me on this incredible life-changing journey, thank you Woodsy and Radar, Brian, Deacon, Iron Horse and Hattie Mae, Carey Lewis, Don and Chris, Katu, Nappy, Me-Tree and You-Tree, Jaberwoki and Love—thank you all for walking with me!

And lastly, I'd like to thank the one person who truly made this journey possible…thank you Jarrett Krentzel. Thank you for bringing me out here. Thank you for believing in yourself. And thank you for *Walking With Pacence.*

This journey has been much more than just a life-changing experience…it's been a full understanding of how one can truly change their life!

I thank nature for teaching me this change.

Harmony to all—Pacence

P.S.—You-Tree, this is for you…I finally figured out the answer to our question:

How many thru-hikers does it take to screw in a light bulb?
Just 1.
As long as they believe they can do it!

A White Blaze

STATE OF MAINE

•

BAXTER STATE PARK
AN AREA OF 116,288 ACRES (1945)

DONATED TO THE STATE OF MAINE BY
PERCIVAL PROCTOR BAXTER
GOVERNER 1921-1924

FOREVER TO BE HELD BY SAID STATE AS TRUSTEE IN TRUST FOR THE BENEFIT OF THE PEOPLE OF MAINE,

1—FOR STATE FOREST, PUBLIC PARK AND PUBLIC RECREATIONAL PURPOSES,

2—AS A SANCTUARY FOR WILD BEASTS AND BIRDS WHERE THE USE OF FIRE-ARMS FOREVER SHALL BE PROHIBITED,

3—AND SAID AREA FOREVER IS TO BE LEFT IN ITS NATURAL WILD STATE IN WHICH NO ROADS OR WAYS FOR MOTOR OR OTHER VEHICLES ARE TO BE CONSTRUCTED AND ON WHICH AIR-CRAFT ARE FORBIDDEN TO LAND; AND THE SAME

4—FOREVER SHALL BE NAMED **BAXTER STATE PARK**

Baxter State Park

DAY 161
Journal Entry—
September 22

Just read a register entry from Iron Horse and Hattie Mae. They made it! Together and happy. Their words were filled with nothing but excitement and delight! I am so happy for them. Back at Gooch Gap Shelter, I wished them both all the blessings to a truly magical flight to wherever their destination may be. Back then, I wished them both the ease of a flight to that of a hawk…and it looks like my wish came true!

The weather down here has been pretty stormy all day, so the park rangers have seriously discouraged any thru-hiker from climbing up Mount Katahdin today. I'm taking my last 0-day here in Baxter State Park before I summit my final mountain tomorrow. I can't believe tomorrow at this time I would have thru-hiked the Appalachian Trail…and at the same time, I totally can. What a journey it has been!

Peace to all.

Goodnight to everything.

MOUNT KATAHDIN

MAN IS BORN TO DIE. HIS WORKS ARE SHORT LIVED.
BUILDINGS CRUMBLE, MONUMENTS DECAY, WEALTH VANISHES
BUT KATAHDIN IN ALL ITS GLORY FOREVER SHALL REMAIN
THE MOUNTAIN OF THE PEOPLE OF MAINE.

P.P.B.

KATAHDIN

BAXTER PEAK   ELEVATION—5267 FT
NORTHERN   TERMINUS   OF   THE
APPALACHIAN   TRAIL

A MOUNTAIN FOOTPATH EXTENDING OVER
2000 MILES TO SPRINGER MTN. GEORGIA

← THOREAU SPRING	1.0 M
← KATAHDIN STREAM CAMPGROUND	6.2
← PENOBSCOT WEST BRANCH AT ABOL BRIDGE	14.5
← MAINE-NEW HAMPSHIRE STATE LINE	281.4
← MT. WASHINGTON, N.H.	332.4
← SPRINGER MTN., GEORGIA	2160.2

MAINE APPALACHIAN TRAIL CLUB

The Northern Terminus of the Appalachian Trail

I DID IT!

From:	Jackie
To:	Friends & Family
Subject:	KATAHDIN
Date:	Monday, September 23, 2002, 5:18pm

Here's the final email from Pacence.
Enjoy, and love.
—Jackie

I DID IT!

I walked from Springer Mountain, Georgia to Mount Katahdin, Maine. I've walked a total distance of roughly 2,160-miles by foot, while allowing my mind and heart to travel much further.

Final words…well, I have none. I had a hard time finding the words to explain why I was going to hike this trail 6-months ago, and I still haven't found the words to explain why I did it 6-months later. I have no words, nothing to say, nothing more to write, nothing else to talk about right now…but I do have this…I have smiles, and hugs, and kisses, and pictures, and memories, and an experience of a lifetime, and courage, and determination, and passion, and stronger legs, and a full beard, and trail-families, and inspiration, and excitement, and the willingness to apply all of these wonderful lessons that I have learned along the way back in society, and I have love…and now, I walk away from this experience with the most important thing I will always have…myself!

Thank you all for following me these past months, whether it was on a map, or reading these emails, or talking with friends, or in your hearts. Thank you all. Knowing that you all were behind me on this trail kept pushing me the whole way through.

Now…I'm in the final trail-town…Millinosket, Maine. Time to celebrate! Tomorrow, I'm driving a truck back to its owner in Andover, Maine. He left his truck at Baxter State Park, where Mount Katahdin is, and I'm doing him this favor. It works out for me as well, for he will then be driving me to wherever I need to go from there. Probably Bangor or Portland, Maine. From there, I'll be getting a ride somehow down to Boston to celebrate with Jackie. And soon, I'll be on my way back home to Hicksville, New York…to get ready for my next adventure, which is already in the works!

Thanks again to all of you, and I'm looking forward to sharing some experiences with you all in the near future.

Peace—love—harmony—Pacence

—AFTER THE TRAIL—

Newsday Newspaper Article (written by Caryn Eve Murray in the Long Island Life section)—
Sunday, November 24, 2002

Home for the Holiday

Growing up in Jericho and Hicksville with the expectations of a suburban lifestyle and corporate life awaiting him somewhere down the road, Jarrett Krentzel recently opted for the road less traveled.

It wasn't even a paved road. For that matter, it was hardly a road at all.

DISCOVERY

Last April, with 60 pounds of camping provisions on his back, Krentzel, 25, set off alone on the 2,000-plus miles of the Appalachian Trail, from its rustic Georgia beginnings to its terminus on a mountaintop in Baxter State Park, Maine. For Krentzel, it was to become a 5½-month spiritual pilgrimage, which no previous travels—Israel when he was 16, Spain and the Sahara Desert during college and work with community nonprofits in the Pacific Northwest—could provide.

"It was to find and define what it is that I believe in life," he said. "And I thought the best way to communicate with myself was through experience." The first 500 miles, he said, were dominated by physical challenges:

"The ankles would go, the back, the shoulders. My body was confronted with a decision—continue breaking down or build yourself back up to be a hiker."

By the time he reached Pennsylvania, he was a hiker.

By the next 500 miles he said, he also was a survivor—so self-assured that he shipped all but 5 pounds of his provisions back home. "Now it had nothing to do with hiking on a trail, but surviving with the most simple resources available," he said.

The journey's end on Sept. 23 brought him back to Long Island—"from one extreme lifestyle to the next," he said. Now working as a naturalist for BOCES, Krentzel is set for a shorter, more conventional journey—his sister's house in Massachusetts for Thanksgiving. "I am not going to treat this Thanksgiving any different than I am going to treat any other day for the rest of my life," he said. "Every day now will be a day of celebration and giving thanks."

He also knows he is home for the holidays—wherever he may be.

"My place is much larger now than just a town or country. Home," he said, "is wherever I am."

Pathways Newsletter Article (The official publication of the New York State Outdoor Education Association)—
Winter, 2003

—The Trees Simply Don't Care—
By: Jarrett 'Pacence' Krentzel: simply another human.

Hello. I would like to begin with sharing my sincere thanks for reading this article. I believe you will enjoy what I have to share with you, and I hope that you can relate to and understand the experiences that I have lived. Most importantly, if you have not done so already, I wish that you will someday experience the harmony and love I have encountered with our Mother Earth.

My trail-name was Pacence (PACEnce). I introduced myself as Pacence, and I was called upon as Pacence for 5 beautiful months. For just about a half of a year, I walked my way from the bold Springer Mountain of Georgia, in Amicalola State Park, to the inspiring Mount Katahdin of Maine, in Baxter State Park. My journey took me along the 2,168 miles of the adventurous Appalachian Trail.

April 15, 2002, I left my home in Hicksville, I left Long Island, and I left New York. I left my family, my friends, my job, my daily chores, my weekly routine, and my monthly schedule. I left all of my responsibilities. I left my watch, my calendar, my car, my bedroom and bed, my bathroom and shower, my kitchen and refrigerator, my living room and TV, my hallway and family photos, my front door, my welcome mat, and my driveway. I left the streets, the stop signs, the traffic lights, the electrical wires, the buildings, the homes, the parking lots, the stores, the offices, the schools, the libraries, the police stations and fire houses, the grocery stores, and the malls. I left the suburban lifestyle. I left it all. I left society as I knew it, and I left it all behind. And on April 15, 2002, I began my initial ascent into the mountains of Georgia, into the woods, into the wilderness, into nature, into the rivers, into the trees, into the mountains and into the hills and into the valleys. I began my ascent into the animals and into the plants, into the waterfalls and into the streams and into the lakes, into the rocks and into the roots and into the soil, into the sunrises and the sunsets and into the moonrises and the moonsets, and into the stars, into the planets, and into myself! On that spring day, I walked out of the world, and *in to* the earth. And I didn't walk out until 5 months later!

What to say, what to write, how do I start? Where do I start, what do I even write about, how can I even explain what happened to me out there, and how will you even understand my experiences? The trees don't care! They don't. *The trees simply don't care.* That's all I can honestly say. When I use the word 'care', I'm not referring to an act of passion, but more to an act of judgment. So when I write that the trees don't care, what I really mean is that the trees don't judge. They don't judge what you say, what you do, what you wear, how you smell, how much money you make, where you live, what you drive, where you shop, what your body looks like, what's on your mind, what's in your heart, what inspires your soul. The trees just don't care. And not only do they not care, but they are also always there for you. They are always there standing tall and strong, ready to be embraced at any moment. They are always there for you to lean on, to sit up against, to shade you, to feed you, to protect you, to nurture you, to teach you, to love you. The trees are always there for you, and they simply do not judge anything. Now that's unconditional love!

Now imagine walking with these trees, mile after mile, hour after hour, day after day, week after week, month after month, still walking with the trees, more miles, more hours, more days, more weeks, more months, and you're still walking, still walking, still living with the trees—the tress who are always there for you and who simply don't care. Now, just imagine how one is eventually affected after walking with the trees for so many miles, day after day, with this understanding of the tree's unconditional acceptance. Just take a moment to imagine the filtration that occurs from the trees into your body, into your mind, right into your heart, and exploding into your soul. Just imagine our trees as our role models, our heroes, our mentors. Imagine all of us looking up to

the trees. You, I, all of us out there, soon became trees! It happened to everyone. Everyone at different points of the trail, but it happened to everyone. And it hit us all like a pile of bricks falling out of the sky, but just before those bricks came crashing onto your head, at that exact point, they all froze up in midair, just an inch away from your head, and when you looked up at those imaginary bricks, you let out a long powerful breath of refreshing air, and poof! They all disappear into thin air, right before your very eyes. And it is then when you've become a tree. It happens just like that. And from that moment on, you free yourself from it all, you become completely liberated, you become totally spontaneous, you live and act on every impulse, and every impulse is positive and loving and wonderful, and you begin to shine, shine, you shine just like the trees do. Your soul shines with passion and love, because now *you* simply don't care. You don't judge anymore. Just like the trees, you stop judging! You stop judging everything and everyone, and most importantly, you stop judging yourself! You don't judge what people say, what people do, what people wear, how people smell, how much money people make, where people live, what people drive, where people shop, what people's bodies look like, what's on people's minds, what's in people's hearts, what inspires people's souls. You just don't care anymore. And with this, you are now all accepting, and you are now always there for everyone and everything. Now, it is you who stands tall and strong. And now it is you who is always ready to embrace everyone and everything at any time. And that's when trail-life really begins!

When this happens, you now feel refreshed, you feel renewed, you feel like you've just cracked open your shell and you begin to run free and wild and naked with Mother Earth. And we did—we all did! Because we all experienced this higher awareness that we all always knew about and that we all still know. It's the awareness that we are all one. The awareness that there is no difference between us as people, and there is no difference between us and the trees and the birds and the plants and the animals and the sunrises and the sunsets and the rocks and the roots and the soil, and there is no difference between ourselves and our Mother Earth. What was so inspiring out there was that we have always known about this awareness…we've all read books, watched movies, listened to songs, listened to people, and learned from other sources that we were all one. But out on the trail, we weren't reading, we weren't watching, we weren't listening…it was a different kind of learning…we were experiencing! We were all experiencing the beauty and harmony of being one with ourselves and with each other and with everything around us. We were experiencing it, and it was real, and we were alive, and it was beautiful, and it was…LOVE!

Five months later, after I made my initial ascent into the mountains of Georgia and into the earth, five months later, on September 23, 2002, I walked down from Mount Katahdin, and into the streets of Maine and into the world. And now I'm back. I'm back with society as I once knew it. I'm back with it all again. I'm back with the suburban lifestyle. I'm back with the malls, the grocery stores, the police stations and fire houses, the libraries, the schools, the offices, the stores, the parking lots, the homes, the buildings, the electrical wires, the traffic lights, the stop signs, and the streets. I'm back with my driveway, my welcome mat, my front door, my hallway and family photos, my living room and TV, my kitchen and refrigerator, my bathroom and shower, my bedroom and bed, my car, my calendar, and my watch. I'm back with all my responsibilities. I'm back with my monthly schedule, my weekly routine, my daily chores, my job, my friends, and my family. I'm back in New York, back on Long Island, and back to my home in Hicksville. And now, I'm ready to journey forward with everything I have just experienced!

Thank you all for giving me the opportunity to share this experience with you. It has been difficult, and it continues to be difficult, to try to find the exact words to explain what has happened to me out there. But after writing all that I have written, I realize that there is still only one way to sum it all up… *The trees simply don't care!*

Harmony to all—Pacence

—4 YEARS, 5 MONTHS, 2 WEEKS & 5 DAYS—

later

Journal Entry—
May 19, 2007

—IMAGINE—

Imagine one day
Everything pauses
Love reaches down
Touches you
Unpauses you
Lifts you up
And shows you something that
No eye can see
No ear can hear
No nose can smell
No tongue can taste
No hand can touch.

Imagine experiencing something that
Only your *self* can feel.

Now imagine
Love places you back down
Reaches back up
Unpauses everything
And resumes life.

What would you say?
What would you think?
What would you write?

WALKING WITH PACENCE

—A True Journey—

Pacence

"To be patient is to be peaceful. To be peaceful is to be at peace with oneself. And to be at peace with myself is to hike my own hike, walk my own walk, journey my own journey—pace my own self—and to pace my own self, is to walk with PACEnce!"—and the moment I experienced the feeling of my trail-name, that's essentially what I continued walking with...I continued Walking With Pacence."

978-0-595-39547-7
0-595-39547-3

Printed in the United States
200581BV00001B/1-90/A